BAD CHILDREN
Can Happen to
GOOD PARENTS

A Survival Manual for
Parents of Difficult Children

by
Norman E. Hoffman
Ph.D., Ed.D., LMFT, LMHC

VG PRESS (A Division of Hoffman Institute (HI)

ISBN 0-9792476-0-8
ISBN 978-0-9792476-0-6

Published in the United States of America
Publisher:
VG PRESS (A Division of Hoffman Institute (HI)
Ormond Beach, FL

Bad Children Can Happen to Good Parents

BAD CHILDREN
Can Happen to
GOOD PARENTS

A Survival Manual for
Parents of Difficult Children

Bad Children Can Happen to Good Parents

Contents

Bad Children Can Happen to Good Parents

Dedication

My wife, Valerie, is my personal blessing, my safe harbor, and the one who has provided the strength and inspiration for me to stay with the arduous task of completing this book. It is with my deepest sincerity and love that I dedicate this book to her.

Bad Children Can Happen to Good Parents

Acknowledgements

I offer my thanks and greatest admiration to my children who have taught me how to be patient but persistent. Each has taught me how to listen and expand my horizons.

Finally, I owe a great deal of gratitude to my wife, Valerie. Without her tireless efforts in reviewing each draft, her analysis of my thoughts and theoretical discussions, and her devotion to my work, the publication of this book never would have been possible.

IMPORTANT

The term "bad children" in my title refers to children with varying degrees of bad or difficult behavior. It is not meant to describe any children as incorrigibly wicked. Throughout this book, I refer to youngsters with specific behavioral challenges as uncaring children.

In my clinical opinion, people are born with a variety of genetic predispositions. From birth, some carry certain genetic predisposed markers that can produce bad behaviors. From a therapeutic standpoint, I believe that all children, regardless of their genetic make-up, can show positive advancements in their behaviors. Their progress can be aided by their parents' affection, perseverance, consistency, and use of an effective technique for the improvement of their children.

Norman E. Hoffman, Ph.D.

Bad Children Can Happen to Good Parents

Preface

Bad Children Can Happen to Good Parents: A Survival Manual for Parents of Difficult Children offers hope for parents who have been forced to accept guilt for the antisocial behavior of their children. It is a manual that challenges not only classical and modern psychology, but also puts an end to the popular myth, "There are no bad children, only bad parents."

Readers will be introduced to the "Uncaring Child Syndrome" and "uncaring children." These terms are used interchangeably to characterize children who lack bonding and generally are disconnected from their caretakers. Uncaring children lack a sense of guilt and remorse. They blame others for their problems, misconducts, and behaviors. They are skillful manipulators who demonstrate a fixed pattern of blatant hostility, selfishness, irresponsibility, and callousness.

Many uncaring children are commonly diagnosed with Oppositional Defiant Disorder and other conduct maladies. Although these diagnoses define some of the behavioral traits of children, uncaring children also have some of the character traits of adult antisocial personality disorder. Therefore, diagnosing "uncaring children" requires specific data to diagnose this condition accurately.

Finally, help is available. Dr. Norman E. Hoffman – a highly regarded psychotherapist, president of the National Board of Forensic Evaluators, and a board-certified mental health counselor specializing in the needs of problem children – gives us relief in knowing that bad children can happen to good parents. Now, there is help and hope for those parents who are seeking to correct the maladaptive behavior of their children.

V. G. Watt, Ph.D., LCSW

Bad Children Can Happen to Good Parents

In the Beginning: A Fable

The roars of the saber-tooth tigers and the wails of the triceratops dinosaurs were nightmarish tales told by two frightened lovers. Both were bewildered and fearful as they sat by the fire and tightly held each other. Their dreams added to an already dreadful and unpleasant evening.

Confronted by their oldest son's defiant and belligerent behavior, they felt that they would never be able to curb his problematic conduct. This night, like many others, was filled with long hours of discussion between the couple. They were frustrated, angry, and apprehensive about what was to become of their ungrateful and ungovernable son. His continued lying, stealing, and disrespectful behavior made it impossible for them to feel comfortable, secure, or positive when it came to their concerns for his future. "What if our younger son grows up to be like him? Can he be helped?" Their many lengthy discussions, their attempts to discipline him, and their abundance of love failed to make any change.

They felt like failures in their rearing of Cain. They searched every element of their child's early development to uncover even the slightest hint of their failure as parents. They recalled how easily he became bored with play. They recalled his jealousy towards his younger brother when the newborn arrived, the fights over sharing his toys, and the fits of anger when he felt that he was being treated unfairly.

They began to ask why their younger son, Abel, was such a model son. Adam was reminded by Eve about how he had said, "Oh, Eve, stop exaggerating. He's just going through a phase. He'll grow out of it." Seemingly annoyed, Adam stood up and walked pensively to the cave entrance. Eve followed and put her arms around him. As Adam turned, he considered the question seriously. "Well, if it is not a phase, what is it? We must have messed up somehow. It doesn't make sense. Ever since I can remember, Abel has been such a good boy, so well behaved, such a gentleman. So, what happened with his brother? He was born shortly before Abel, lives in the same place, has all of the same opportunities, and shares us as his parents. However, it seems that he does not care much about anyone or anything. What went wrong?"

Finally, Eve walked to the spot where Cain was sleeping and began to weep. Adam joined her and gently nudged her to go back to sleep. Eve said, "There must be something that we can do. I'm worried that something bad is about to happen. Cain shows no involvement with or concern for our family. He never shows guilt for what he has done. He seems so jealous and envious of Abel. We had so many dreams of a healthy and happy family. What have we done wrong? What can we do? Why does he behave as he does? I do not know what to do. One day, Cain seems so loving; the next day, he is like a stranger – someone without feeling or caring. The other day, I saw a look on Cain's face that frightened me. While Abel was planting flowers in the garden, Cain hit him with a rock. While laughing, he ran off with that damn pet snake that goes everywhere with him. Although he said that it was an accident, I know differently. It was no accident."

"Eve, that's ridiculous. In spite of his problem behavior, I can't believe that he would ever intentionally hurt his brother."

"But, Adam, there's something wrong with that boy. There's been something wrong with him ever since I can remember!"

Chapter 1:
Am I Losing My Child?

"Youth is disintegrating. The youngsters of the land have disrespect for their elders and contempt for authority in every form. Vandalism is rife, and crime of all kinds is rampant among our young people. The nation is in peril."

Priest in Egypt, 2,000 BC

We are befuddled and feel totally helpless as we watch many of our children slip from our protection, our families, and us. They seem uncaring, unloving, and alien. They resist our pleas to stop destructive behaviors that seem without goals and void of good judgment, remorse, or caring feelings. Their defiance, selfishness, lack of learning from experience, superficiality, and broken promises increase, while our own hopes that they will improve become unrealistic fantasies.

By the time that some of our children turn eight, we as parents can hardly believe their dramatic personality changes and behaviors that go far beyond the boundaries of expected adolescent yearnings. We become conscious of their marked lack of guilt or remorse and their failure to deal with anything that may make them anxious.

Suddenly, we feel like we are at war. But who is the enemy? Is it the parents because they are guilty of inadequate parenting? Do we not have the skills to understand and communicate with our children? Is our society so overwhelmed with stress that we are unable to meet the needs of our children?

As in any war, the pain and suffering are intense and both sides suffer tremendously. Some of the most caustic wounds and the most significant losses are inflicted upon those whose lives are touched by the children. With self imposed prophesies of pain, these children are leaving legacies of costs and sorrows to those around them. If we ignore the unquestionable fact that our kids could be in trouble in a troubled world and if we fail to confront this tragic condition with a new set of rules and parenting skills, the loss of our children is inevitable.

The trend in the United States has been to view children as basically good entities whose behavior is molded from a blueprint drawn by the architects of the family: the parents. In the past when a child misbehaved, we looked at the parents as the culprits. Most writers and therapists still place the blame of children going bad on the environment or on the parents – or both. In 1962, Arthur Thomas Jersild, author of The Psychology of Adolescents and books on education wrote, "This contrasts with some earlier speculations to the effect that criminal tendencies are inherited – the criminal springs from 'bad seed.' Actually, no delinquent has a gene – or a set of genes that produced in him a tendency to steal a horse or a car."

As parents, we believe that we or the environment is at fault because that is what we have been told. We have been taught to think that we are not providing proper care and love, that we lack listening skills, and that our actions have possibly damaged or retarded our children's normal development. Naturally, this belief causes guilt and self recrimination in what may be an already-disintegrated family. But often, regardless of how hard we try to find remedies, our children remain unresponsive and become even more problematic.

In 1965, Haim Ginott (p. 107), renowned psychologist, wrote of the costly consequences of an unhappy childhood. He stated, "We are deeply concerned lest we damage our children for life." He said, "She [the mother of the child] would be more helpful if she had less guilt and more skill."

Stanton Samenow (p. 48), author of Inside the Criminal Mind, suggested that there are kids who will "inflict enormous damage upon society" regardless of what their parents do. Initially, Samenow believed that criminal behavior was symptomatic of internal conflicts caused by early childhood trauma and deprivation. From his experience and research, he had to unlearn everything that he had learned about the causation of criminal behavior. He then concluded that new methods are necessary to deal with these difficult children. His new approach reasons that criminals choose to commit crimes.

It may be that these children's perception of the world is faulty. A 1978 study by Leonard Savitz and Norma Johnson (p. 16), authors of

Crime in Society, stated, "There is little doubt that bad people see the world differently from good."

Sal

Sal, an eleven year old preadolescent boy, had been suspended three times for fighting and talking back to his sixth-grade teacher. He lived with his mother, stepfather, and eight year old sister. Ever since he was in the first grade, teachers indicated that Sal had difficulty in keeping his mind on schoolwork, disobeyed the rules, had frequent temper outbursts, was moody, and seemed to like playing the role of class clown. After being called to school repeatedly because of Sal's misconduct, his parents sought the help of a family counselor. The expenses in time and money mounted as the family counselor advised them to "win Sal's cooperation" by planning family outings and involving Sal in weekly family meetings to discuss problems and relevant issues. The counselor suggested that they try to be more reflective (a therapeutic skill introduced by psychologist Carl Rogers circa 1951) in their listening skills and less authoritative, while treating the boy with equality and using "I-messages." An I message is a communication technique used by Don Dinkmeyer, author of Systematic Training for Effective Parenting (STEP), that helps each participant to share feelings and concerns in a non-threatening and nonjudgmental manner. Discouraged and beaten, the parents terminated the treatment after several months.

When I first became involved in the mental health profession in 1963, the practice at that time was – and continues to be – the standard intervention technique offered to most parents with similarly troubled children. Therapeutic literature is filled with the notion that a problem child is the fault of the parents. The implication is that the identified problem child is not the primary person who is responsible for the family's conflict – a premise that is the hallmark of family counseling and that focuses the blame on the parents. This concept unfortunately results from the modern day belief that "There are no bad children, only bad parents," a teaching that singularly has caused needless guilt and delay in family progress and the parenting process.

When attempting to deal with problem children throughout the years, parents have been left immobilized and powerless to cope with and improve family conflict. Their ineffectiveness is largely due to the lack of the understanding of the Uncaring Child Syndrome (UCS) by mental health professionals. Their attempts to help the family usually take the form of accusing good parents of being traumatizing and "bad," thereby frustrating any possibility of their child's healthy development if changes are not made. Parents are left with undeserved guilt and self reproach that make positive change impossible.

The belief that good parents can have bad children is generally unacceptable by the population at large. To suggest its possibility also might imply a complete breakdown in the time honored beliefs in the "sanctity" of children who theoretically are all born good and only become bad because of parental and environmental influences.

But what if there were children whose behavior is influenced primarily by their own selfish, single minded needs to achieve pleasure and self gratification with little or no regard for others? These children would have no bonding with their parents or siblings, would blame others for their own failures, and rarely, if ever, would have insight into their behavior.

Such children do exist. They see themselves as gentle and caring in their manipulative attempts to get involved with other human beings. Unfortunately, their tremendous inadequacies make developing healthy, meaningful, and lasting relationships impossible. What at first may look like close involvements and commitments are really the masquerades of intimate relationships. For instance, they may overly generalize philosophical statements, which initially may be interpreted as wisdom but later will be found to be major barriers in communication. Sal, mentioned previously, is a prime example. These same children also may indulge in excessive drinking, drug usage, gambling, manipulation, sexual deviation, and violence. These behaviors make them feel adequate and fulfilled – at least temporarily. However, since they are unable to maintain lasting and meaningful relationships, their self esteem and identities become increasingly and constantly threatened.

The family is usually the most vulnerable target and the most frequent contact for the manipulation of uncaring children because of their power and control over the ones who have the most to lose. During my many years of conducting counseling, I've learned that the one who has invested the most in a relationship has the least power. In spite of the emotional and physical pain that children repeatedly inflict on their parents, they continue to invest emotionally and physically in their child, their baby. To bear this horrid pain, the parents look to the past for answers and relief. They see their youngsters as the cuddly, cute, and adorable children who smiled, cooed, and positively justified their childrearing. They still see these youngsters as small children who are growing, developing, and fulfilling their own dreams and fantasies within normal, healthy, and loving families. They then make excuses for their children's behaviors and overlook significant cues and opportunities to intervene. These memories (along with tendencies to be blinded when it comes to seeing their children as "bad") and the monumental guilt and self-reproach prolong and feed the flame of the children's unhealthy behaviors. Parents desperately want to believe and forgive. They make new agreements to gain their children's approval.

Unfortunately, they are constantly left frustrated, exasperated, and hopeless with their children's repeated performances of broken promises, lies, thefts, and disobedience of family rules.

As long as children hold power positions in the family system, the youngsters maintain control over the atmosphere, directions, goals, and plans of the family. As the family continues to invest in the hope of connecting with these youngsters, the children's disconnection prevails and brings the family powerlessly to its knees. Parents are reduced to pleading for their children to understand their feelings. They attempt to instill a sense of guilt so that the youngsters will appreciate their pain. Instead, the children avoid them and blame them for the prevailing dilemmas, while demanding further freedom by attempting to be portrayed as victims of constrictive and uncaring parents. These children are masters of fixing the blame on parents, siblings, teachers, and peers. As skillful manipulators, these children can interweave half truths into rational and believable stories, thereby being vindicated from any wrongdoings in their own minds.

Penelope Leach, the author of Children First, stated, "Parents are the victims of monumental social injustice. They are having a lousy time, and it isn't their fault" (Meltz see pp. 1F-2F). She puts the blame for the parents' impotency on society, government, and business policies that do not support parents' needs.

For the purpose of this book – and since antisocial, sociopathic, and psychopathic have virtually the same meaning – the term "antisocial" will be used exclusively to describe these equivalent types of acts. A distinction must be made between antisocial behavior and antisocial criminal behavior. Antisocial behaviors of uncaring children are not socially acceptable, but the children may not necessarily become criminals. For example, an individual who lies, skips school, and is disrespectful may be antisocial, but that person is not necessarily a criminal. While an antisocial act is always involved when a crime is committed, a crime is not always involved when an antisocial act is committed. It is this distinction that separates the antisocial person from the antisocial criminal.

Antisocial Characteristics

Antisocial behaviors are those acts that are ascribed to people who demonstrate a fixed pattern of blatant hostility, selfishness, irresponsibility, and callousness. They have great difficulty in forming significant loyalties to individuals or groups. They behave in ways that often result in legal or social offenses. Unable to learn from experience, such people are resistant to all forms of psychotherapeutic intervention. In 1976, Hervey Cleckley, author of The Mask of Sanity, listed the following characteristics of antisocial behavior:

1. Superficial charm and intelligence
2. Absence of delusions and other signs of irrational thinking
3. Absence of nervousness or psychoneurotic manifestations
4. Unreliability
5. Untruthfulness
6. Lack of remorse or shame
7. Inadequately motivated antisocial behaviors
8. Poor judgment and failure to learn from experience
9. Pathologic egocentricity in the capacity for love
10. General poverty in major affective reactions
11. Specific loss of insight
12. Unresponsiveness in general interpersonal relationships
13. Fantastic and uninviting behavior with drinking and sometimes without drinking
14. Suicide rarely committed after threats
15. Sex life, impersonal, trivial, and poorly integrated
16. Failure to follow any life plan

The interpretation that follows was the hallmark of my earlier thinking when forming a theory to account for antisocial behavior: Until

1982, I accepted the psychoanalytic (deep psychological exploration) theory and held analytic (exploratory) interpretation as sacred. But when I began working with the families of uncaring children in South Florida, I found it difficult to continue in such a rigid and narrow view. I began to treat children whose siblings had no unusual problems with their families, school, or interpersonal relationships.

According to psychoanalytic theory, antisocial personality is rooted during the first fifteen months of life, Chapman (1976). These children are frustrated and confused. They may experience massive rejection by their parents. Upon reaching puberty, these children may suffer from excessive frustration caused by this rejection. This makes it almost impossible for them to form healthy relationships. Very clearly, these children have been massively and continuously traumatized throughout their childhood and they have had difficulties in identifying with a healthy parent. These early conflicts that are unresolved cause severe structural defects in their personality.

Until 1982, I believed that there must be unhealthy developmental factors in the form of inappropriate child rearing, rejection, or separation in order for antisocial behaviors to exist. I also thought that there could not be meaningful and healthy relationships in early development in such cases. But I was bothered by one thing: How could parents raise two or three seemingly healthy children and have only one who is antisocial? What was I missing? Must I dig deeper into early development? Were there family secrets that were being kept from me?

The more important question for me was, "Are we causing unnecessary hardships and monumental guilt for good parents with bad kids?" If the answer is "yes," what characterizes the obvious behaviors of the adolescents who refuse to cooperate and choose to continue in their maladaptive, disruptive, and disturbing actions? Why are there such disparities in the feelings and attitudes of uncaring children? What are the early warning signs? How do they become uncaring? What do they feel? Can they be helped? Whose fault is it that they become this way?

This book attempts to answer these questions and bring better understanding to parents struggling to raise moral and caring children. Evidence shows that an increasing number of children – children who do not necessarily fit into the diagnostic category of antisocial personality and who do not commit criminal acts – engage in behaviors destructive

to themselves and others. Therefore, they do not successfully participate in interpersonal and social relationships, Reid (1978). It is these
children who fit the profile of the Uncaring Child Syndrome.

Chapter 2:
Four Profiles of the
Uncaring Child Syndrome

"Youth is a malady of which one becomes cured a
little every day."

Benito Mussolini
on his fifteenth birthday

THE CHAMELEONS

I refer to some uncaring children as chameleons who, like lizards
that are capable of changing their color, are able to change their disposi-
tions and habits. Their whole relationship to life lacks genuineness and
authenticity. These children do not see anything wrong with themselves
and they are devoid of any traces of warmth. They give the impression of making good adjustments to life, but they actually take on the
personalities of others and copy their ideas and ideals. They are ready
to adopt any and all of other people's attitudes, reactions, and behaviors
that they feel are expected. Thus, they have no real and identifiable
personality. They shift from thing to thing and person to person.

Carrie

Thirteen year old Carrie was brought to me by her parents who
complained that she lied, ran away from home, and was argumentative. Her grades in school were dropping because she was not doing
her homework.

When Carrie was six years old, her parents had been concerned
about their daughter's lack of self motivation in her play. At the same
time, she seemed to become easily bored. In spite of her parent's many
attempts to motivate and interest her in various projects, Carrie's pat-

tern was usually the same. When something new was presented, she at first became excited and enthusiastic, but soon lost interest after a few minutes. There was one notable exception: When Carrie's playmates showed interest in the same thing, her enthusiasm and interest continued. Apparently, copying others energized Carrie's behavior, but, at the same time, she was unable to crystallize and maintain her own identity. She acted as if she had thought of the ideas and projects herself when, in fact, they had come from others.

While her parents spent a lot of time entertaining her in efforts to motivate self interest, they also reported their fear that she never felt remorse or guilt for any of her actions that caused pain to others. She could not be depended upon to complete chores, projects, or any other commitment that she agreed to do in spite of continued talks about responsibility and threats of punishment.

Carrie displayed another important warning sign by refusing to deal with any unpleasant problems that she caused. No matter how often her parents pressed her to discuss and resolve any such conflict, Carrie's usual response was, "I've already dealt with it. It is in the past. Why don't you ever stop talking about the same things?" She lacked empathy, genuineness, and sincere warmth in any relationship that demanded more than a superficial understanding.

Further exploration revealed a girl who had no attachments to her personal belongings. In fact, she gave away, lost, or misused her possessions regardless of her parents' attempts to get her to appreciate them. This lack of regard for her belongings carried over to a blatant lack of concern for other people's property. She would borrow, lose, or misuse her friends' and parents' items with equal disregard.

When Carrie was eight years old, her parents began to hear stories about her from her playmates. They told bizarre tales about how Carrie was unloved, abused, and unwanted by her parents. These lurid lies brought total frustration and tears to loving and caring parents whose daughter was the most cherished person in their lives.

Carrie's profile shows a child with the budding traits of the Uncaring Child Syndrome. She was a child who presented a chameleon-like pretense with no inner substance. This girl seemed to resent and repel all expressions of concern from those who loved her, thus she defied the empathetic understanding and regard that is so necessary for healthy and meaningful relationships to exist. No sense of bonding or connection ever existed between her and her parents or between her and her friends. Ironically, Carrie believed that she was a loving and caring child with many "close and loyal friends." Her reality seemed distorted. She was unable or unwilling to appreciate what others were attempting to elicit from her or make her feel. She could not – or would not – understand their pain or allow herself to be seen as the one who created it.

Jonathan

Jonathan was fourteen when his parents requested my help. When they came to me, they were fearful that their son would run away and possibly become involved in the drug scene. They explained that he was unwilling to do homework, his grades were failing, and he was "hanging around" with peers whom his parents described as undesirable. At home, he watched television excessively, avoided involvement in family activities, disregarded daily chores, and generally lacked interest or motivation in almost all of his daily functions.

Jonathan's parents told me that he had lacked self motivation throughout his life. Whenever his friends expressed any type of interest, Jonathan acted as if he had generated that interest himself. For instance, when Jonathan expressed an enthusiasm in a specific jazz artist, he would passionately discuss the artist and his music. He would purchase many of the artist's recordings and play them for his parents. He seemed to take great delight in demonstrating his interest to his parents, who also expressed happiness in his newly found passion. But they soon discovered that Jonathan's interest actually was the interest of his friend. When his friend's interest waned, so did Jonathan's.

THE OPERATORS

Operators are children who are charming and ingratiating, while being experts at wheeling, dealing, and conning parents and others. Operators display a high degree of dominance and are well liked by their peers. However, they rarely learn from their mistakes. Without concern for others, they relentlessly engage in deceptions for momentary gain.

Lenny

Lenny was a successful twenty five year old individual who expounded on some of his earlier achievements. He boasted of how he was able to sell used pianos and organs to poor people by promising a 100% guarantee. He bragged about never making good on any complaints by maneuvering his company to avoid any possible litigation. A failing marriage and difficulty with his children finally brought him into counseling. During the entire therapy process, Lenny maintained an impenetrable barrier that made any intervention impossible. He was convinced that he was right and everyone else was wrong. His superficial charm, yet lack of insight, made all attempts to change his behavior frustrating. The result of his unbending attitude was the dissolution of his marriage and divorce.

Manny

While treating Manny and Marlene for marital problems, I learned that Manny, a thirty year old insurance agent, had cheated and lied to some of his clients. Although he attempted to present himself as a man of integrity, his wife portrayed him as someone who would con, lie, and steal from anyone. Some positive changes were seen early in therapy, but Manny returned to his previous antisocial behavior when therapy ended. Several additional attempts at marital counseling were uneventful. Manny was a great con man. He had all of the charm and "gift of gab" necessary for his trade. Unfortunately, he had little regard for the rights of others. He felt no shame, guilt, or remorse for his uncaring actions.

Sharon

Sharon was sixteen years old when her parents contacted me. She had been suspended from school because she falsified absences. Sharon would write fraudulent excuses, supposedly signed by her parents, in order to cut school. She accomplished this for almost six months without being discovered and she developed a network of peers to assist her in her elaborate schemes to skip classes. Sharon also had been researching the drug market and asking questions about the sale of drugs. Her school counselor spoke to some of her peers who corroborated this fact.

Sharon was considering becoming a drug dealer by repackaging over the counter caffeine tablets and selling them as pills called "speed." Although she had not committed any criminal act up to that point, she appeared likely to become involved in antisocial criminal acts.

Sharon's parents told me that she liked to be the "boss" as a child. She seemed to have many friends, but she was always the leader. Whenever Sharon was caught doing something wrong, she seemed able to maneuver herself out of the problem. "She had answers for everything," Sharon's parents told me, as they explained her unique ability to change the circumstance of the conflict or even her original statements to make herself appear guiltless. Sharon rarely if ever felt bad when her behavior created havoc for her family. Her lying, stealing, and false promises left her family with tremendous emotional pain.

While investigating the early behavioral tendencies of all of these individuals, I began to see a set of predominate patterns. All of the parents recalled their children's preoccupation with their own pleasures, problems, and self gratification. Some of these kids felt rejected in spite of their family's attempts to develop togetherness. A feeling of bonding, attachment, and a sense of intimacy with parents seldom occurred due to their indifference.

THE HELLBENDERS

Hellbenders are children who behave a little more daringly than their peers do. They appear to take unnecessary risks and are accident-prone. They are the proverbial accident waiting to happen.

Valerie

Valerie was fifteen years old when I initially saw her. She had been suspended from school for rather harmless pranks. When confronted about her behavior, she stated confidently that her teacher had "overreacted" to things that were "minor." She could not understand why the teacher "got on my case." Valerie's pranks, although insignificant, were disruptive behaviors that continued in spite of repeated attempts by her teacher to curtail them. Valerie's similar and repeated problems in other classes prompted the principal to suspend her.

Her parents told me that she was always a child who "went past the point of no return." When she was five, she climbed on furniture to get to the kitchen cabinets. In spite of falling and sustaining injuries on several occasions, this behavior persisted. Throughout her entire childhood, she would place herself in danger regardless of her parents' many warnings. During play, she would run around without regard for the safety of others or herself. She would climb higher on the monkey bars than her peers and swing higher. She delighted in exploring areas of the playground that were off-limits to children of her age.

Barry

Seventeen year old Barry was referred to me by his parents after he had been arrested for driving while intoxicated. They described him as having repeated disciplinary difficulties with school authorities, being truant, and failing at school. He was incorrigible. He fought with his peers and had many encounters with the police because of his reckless driving.

He described his parents as being overly controlling, demanding, and making his life a "living hell." He blamed his teachers for "picking" on him and claimed that the police harassed him. He threatened to leave home so that he would no longer be a bother to anyone.

Barry's parents portrayed him as a "boy with vengeance." They said that he always had created turmoil at home and in the neighborhood when he was growing up. While playing in the house, he would play catch with any object available, regardless of how fragile. He had broken the dining room chandelier by swinging on it after seeing a Tarzan movie. He would place objects in the electrical sockets to see what would happen. His fascination with matches once caused him to set the garage on fire. In spite of his parents' repeated attempts to change his behavior, Barry continued his reckless pursuit.

THE TRANSFORMERS

In the beginning, transformers are the "good children," for all intents and purposes. When parents discuss this child, they say, "He was such a good child." "She did what she was told the first time." "He never gave me any trouble." But, around the age of twelve, the child becomes a markedly different individual who is uncaring and disobedient. The parents cannot understand what has happened to their loving offspring, the cause of this condition, or what to do to change it.

Peter

Peter, at fifteen, came to me because he was disobedient, refused to do homework, failed in school, and verbally assaulted his mother. He also was in love with a seventeen year old girl who was a high school dropout. He wanted to drop out of school when he turned sixteen, leave his parents' home, live with his girlfriend, and work as a laborer.

Peter's parents characterized his childhood as uneventful. They said that his early development had been normal; in fact, he had been the "perfect child." He was an average student and had no unusual problems throughout school. But, when he reached the age of twelve, his parents noticed a shift from being good to being bad. He began to lie about his homework. He cut up in class to the point of being branded the "class clown" and he became disobedient.

His parents made me aware of another peculiar behavior. He began to malign his mother and to display anger and contempt for what he believed was unfair and poor treatment of him by her. Whenever he perceived that he was being denied, he would slander her and become depressed and angry. Every problem that he had at school or at home was blamed on his mother. He got a certain feeling of relief when his disruptive behavior was discovered and he appeared to derive a disturbing pleasure from being discovered and punished.

Although the parents reported nothing unusual about his childhood development, further exploration of his personality traits revealed some interesting facts. Although he had few friends as a child, Peter had been unable to sustain interest in self motivated play. In other words, he became bored easily when playing by himself. He seemed to do better when playing with other children.

I also learned that Peter was a follower. Most of the time, he would join the activities of others and follow their lead. He rarely challenged his peers, but, when he did, he soon disengaged by submitting to others. When Peter reached the age of twelve, he began challenging his mother's position of authority with caustic and demeaning remarks. His behavior progressively had worsened by the time that he was fifteen. It should be noted that he rarely challenged his father.

Peter's girlfriend came into the picture when he turned fifteen. She was characterized as a very strong and dominant individual from a lower social and economic class. Initially, she was described as a "sweet young girl," who was well liked by Peter's parents. After a short time, when Peter's behavior became more combative and argumentative, his parents felt that he was in "her control" and was no longer willing to work out their differences.

Much like the chameleon, Peter appeared to take on his girlfriend's characteristics and mannerisms. His role became strengthened and reinforced by her positive acknowledgments. Being unaware of his personality transformation, he focused his energy more on his "bad mother," whom he saw as overly controlling and guilt-producing.

Susan

Susan, much like Peter, was described as the "perfect child." When she was about thirteen, her parents began to notice changes in her behavior. She lied about her whereabouts and homework. By the time that she was fourteen, she was coming home late from school and from her girlfriend's house. Not only did her lying get progressively worse, but she also became more negative and belligerent with authority figures.

Susan's involvement with her peers seemed to have a profound effect on her transformation. She was described as a child who usually followed the lead of others. When she became involved with older peers, she took on some of their traits and portrayed herself as bad.

If Susan's parents had been more skilled in recognizing the early signs of the transformers, they may have been more effective in mediating and resolving the problem at its onset. Unfortunately, pediatricians, school counselors, and therapists tell most parents that "This is just a phase of development and it will soon pass."

Chapter 3:
DISCOMFORT:
The Catalyst for Change

Most of us have heard that "Boys will be boys."
We must remember that "Boys will be men."

I will be explaining how discomfort, a mild to moderate form of anxiety, can be beneficial in treating uncaring children, but I first want to reveal the intricate nature of anxiety itself.

When I began working with the children at the Devereux Foundation in Devon, Pennsylvania, in 1963, the kids impressed me with their broad spectrum of emotional disturbance and also the degree to which they experienced hurt, rejection, and anxiety.

For example, Joe, a sixteen year old male, was depressed about the divorce of his parents, the subsequent absence of his father, and the rejection by his mother. His mood was sullen and he remained withdrawn from our staff and his peers. Initial attempts to form a relationship with him were met with further withdrawal and a frozen posture. Any confrontation by his peers resulted in heightened anxiety and deepened depression as tears streamed down his cheeks. His face would become flush and his voice tremulous.

The anxiety caused by such emotional pain is unwanted, but it can be treated more successfully because of the nature of its pain. This type of anxiety, called subjective anxiety, stems from people's awareness of their depression, their perceived roles in its cause, the resultant guilt, and the fear of continued emptiness that seems unavoidable (See "Chapman" on page 79). Anxiety is one of the central concepts of interpersonal psychiatry. In 1954, Harry Stack Sullivan, pioneer of the Interpersonal Approach to Psychiatry, employed this term in a special way. By anxiety, he means virtually all of the basic types of emotional suffering. This anxiety includes anxiousness, guilt, shame, dread, feelings of personal worthlessness, and other less definable painful feelings. Anxiety varies in degree from mild discomfort that is scarcely noticeable to disorganizing and incapacitating panic.

As Sullivan emphasized, the basic cause of anxiety is a strong threat to the emotional balance and wellbeing of people, which is a threat to their integrity. Such a threat is the result of emotional turmoil, both within people and in their relationships with others. This turmoil is caused by traumatic interpersonal relationships in both past and present life situations. As people sense that their emotional stability is being menaced – or even crumbling – they are flooded by profound feelings of dread and apprehension that we call anxiety (See "Chapman" on pages 78-86).

The symptoms associated with subjective anxiety in its severe form include increased heart activity, sweating, disturbed breathing, dizziness, apprehension, and feelings of impending doom. Obviously, this is a picture that anyone would want removed. Subjective anxiety is unwanted, frightening, and persistent. It creates pain and suffering for those afflicted.

Another cause of depression and subjective anxiety is in the notion of hidden guilt. Some children emerge from their childhood with profound inner turmoil caused by one or more traumatic events or unhealthy relationships that led to the formation of overwhelming guilt. They experience symptoms of anxiety, but have no idea about what may be the cause. They may evidence heart palpitations, cold sweaty palms, hyperventilation, tremulous hands, facial muscular tension, and feelings of imminent death. However, these obvious signs of inner turmoil and severe outward distress actually make a more positive treatment possible.

Adolescents who are reprimanded by their teachers for misbehaving may experience insecurity, rejection, and distress from their perceived threats or may feel anger and dislike for the perceived criticisms. In any case, the adolescents may become uneasy by their newly shaken security and the unknown consequences of their actions. It is within this new framework that the anxiety flourishes.

Another cause of anxiety should be obvious in the following example: The parents of a fourteen year old girl grounded her for not doing her homework, lying, and producing poor grades. The girl's first response was anger and withdrawal from her family. However, because of some understanding but firm parental intervention, she began to express remorse and humiliation for doing so poorly and she acknowledged the reality of her responsibility. She expressed fear about the loss of her parents' love. Her manifest anger and withdrawal was a defense against experiencing further rejection and guilt. When her parents talked to her about their love for her and demonstrated that they would not accept her misbehavior, the fourteen year old's manifest guilt, anxiety, and fear of loss emerged.

A child who fails to experience subjective anxiety rarely will understand or appreciate family pain and the need for cooperation and change. This child feels only the pain of the moment, which lasts only as long as the conflict is paramount. As soon as the pressure is diminished, they resume their pattern of irresponsibility and indifference.

Contrary to subjective anxiety and its positive prognosis for treatment, the uncaring adolescent experiences another kind of anxiety: objective anxiety. The uncaring person indeed experiences anxiety, but it is "the anxiety of the moment" and it lasts only as long as the perceived threat is present. They may be awaiting a hearing for a legal infraction, wondering if their parents will discover their lying, or hiding their failing grades. This objective anxiety subsides as soon as the threat is gone. If anxiety lasts only for the moment and the person is able to escape uncomfortable situations without regard or remorse for those whom they have hurt, one can quickly understand the difficulty in helping this individual to work on mediating and resolving interpersonal conflicts.

When we think about behavioral or emotional problems of children, we become concerned with a multitude of issues. Are the parents properly caring for these children? Are they suffering emotional, physical, or sexual abuse? Are they depressed? However, how often do we consider the widespread emotional and physical abuse that children can perpetrate on their parents? To understand the immense suffering of the family, we must first recognize the parents' and family members' attempts to help the uncaring child, in spite of continued rejection, alienation, and abuse by the child. This can be better understood by the following examples of June and John:

June

June was a seventeen year old whom her father described as a "pathological liar." Other than detecting her lying behavior, her parents always had seen her as warm and loving. However, they now were questioning whether she really cared at all. They had lost their trust in anything that June said. They also experienced a loss in their ability to love her as they had in the past.

June revealed a significant piece of information that has become a cornerstone in assessing similar individuals. This dialogue illustrates:

Therapist: "Why did you feel you had to falsify your teacher's signatures on your progress report?"

June: "I didn't want to get punished."

Therapist: "Punished?"

June: "Yeah! You see, my mom and dad would yell and never let up."

Therapist: "So, you forged the signatures not to get yelled at?"

June: "Yeah."

Therapist: "Do you recall the last family session when your parents reminded you that they never yell or punish you when you tell the truth and you agreed?"

June: "Well, I guess so."

Therapist: "When you learned your father contacted the school about your progress report, what did you feel? Were you frightened about being found out?"

June: "Not really. You see, I knew I could talk my way out of it when I got home. So, I really wasn't worried."

Therapist: "I understand you discovered your father contacted the school in the morning. Was there any fear at all during the rest of the school day?"

June: "No. Why should I be afraid? I knew I could get out of it. It was completely out of my mind. When I got home, I was a little nervous, but that didn't get in the way of talking to my dad."

Therapist: "So you continued to lie in spite of knowing your parents were informed of the truth?"

June: "Yeah! That may sound dumb, but I've done it before – and got away with it."

This dialogue is typical of children like June. They show disregard for values and principles and do not experience the anxiety that normally would be expected. The subsequent sessions with June were uneventful. She continued to view therapy as a "waste of time" while attempting to diminish her wrongdoing. Therapy then was directed to working with her parents. The task was the diminishing of the parents' anxiety and the placement of the anxiety in the form of controlled discomfort onto June. The parents and therapist/counselor determine the degree of discomfort based on the particular needs of the child. Without June's experience of discomfort, positive change could not be expected. When children are resistant to working through the problems that they cause, I find it more useful to direct my attention to the parents. When parents have the tools to facilitate change in their children, more positive outcomes may be expected.

Dealing with June's lack of concern or anxiety in any form was the focus of my therapeutic attention. After proposing a plan to make June responsible for her actions and consequences, I noted the initial progress. Progress was interrupted because June ran off with her boyfriend. Her parents continued to feel guilt and emotional pain due to their perceived failure. They blamed themselves for not being able to resolve June's problems earlier.

June was not bothered by nor was able to identify with any type of anxiety in spite of her parent's confrontation. This missing link – discomfort, a mild to moderate form of anxiety – must be present before any meaningful behavioral changes can be made. Working on changing misbehavior should be started as early as it is noticed.

John

A school counselor referred thirteen-year-old John to me. John's parents reported an array of problematic behaviors that had begun in the first grade. His current problems included disobeying teachers, instigating fights, walking out of class, using profanity, refusing to obey family rules or to do chores, lacking concern for the rights of others, and making poor grades. John's eleven year old brother was a good student who had no problems at home or school and who easily formed and maintained interpersonal relationships.

John's parents worked in middleclass jobs and adequately provided for all of their children's emotional and material needs. Both parents had come from healthy and caring parents with whom they maintained close relationships. There was nothing noteworthy in either parent's past that would suggest family pathology. Both parents entered into marriage with hopes of raising healthy children and providing them with all of the love and guidance that they could give. They were not ready or prepared for what was to occur. The parents reported nothing unusual during John's first six years of life. When he entered the first grade, they began getting reports from the teacher about his stubbornness, oppositional behavior, and inattentiveness. This scenario continued throughout elementary school. He was suspended four times for fighting, being disobedient, and cursing. His parents said that John was untrustworthy, aggressive, and a liar. He stole money from them, violated the rules at home, and had temper outbursts. When angry, he threw and broke things.

After repeated attempts to change John's maladaptive behaviors, his parents engaged a mental health professional to counsel John and the family. The counselor insisted that the parents needed to be less restrictive and should allow their child to have more freedom for self-expression. He encouraged reflective listening techniques and I-messages so that they might win his cooperation. After three months of therapy, the family dropped out of treatment because they saw no meaningful change in his behavior.

Two more attempts at therapy were also unsuccessful. School personnel regularly contacted John's parents about his repeated problematic behavior. John's mother had to make excuses to her boss so that she could leave work to deal with her son's troubles at school.

As the problems continued without resolution, a rift between the parents began to widen due to the perceived softening or hardening of discipline by either parent. As John's behavior became the predominant focus of daily attention, the atmosphere in the home became cold and unfriendly. His brother became more isolated and absent in family matters. Due to John's rude and uncaring attitude, the maternal grandparents experienced additional emotional pain when they came for a visit during a two week vacation.

The family was in severe conflict and experienced significant pain, loss, frustration, and disillusionment. John's uncaring and indifferent attitude toward their despair further aggravated an already miserable and decaying situation. Nevertheless, they continued to make every effort to reach him and make him feel their pain. Unfortunately, their attempts were in vain. In fact, their repeated and fruitless attempts not only caused further turmoil and despair, but they reinforced their powerlessness to an already power mad John. He remained fully in charge of the emotional health of the family. In spite of John's continued alienation from his relatives, they repeatedly but futilely expended emotional and physical energy to get him to behave in a caring and unselfish manner.

To understand the nature and extent of these horrifying problems, we must recognize the conditions that apparently foster and nurture their existence and perpetuation. To illustrate this, let us look at the case of one thirteen year old female patient who did not arrive at home from school at her scheduled time. Her frantic parents spent the next two hours calling the school, neighbors, and her friends. Finally, they received a phone call from their babysitter, who was several miles from their home. She informed them that their daughter was with her. The child told them that she had been held down by several boys on the bus and was prevented from exiting. However, her friends revealed that the child missed her stop because she had been playing and "cutting up" with her girlfriends and several boys. Upon confrontation, she denied what her friends had reported and began to make further accusations about their character. It was not until her best friend and her parents confronted the child that she broke down and admitted her action. However, even after her admission, she accused her parents, friends, and schoolmates of hating her. She held fast to a tale of never being cared about or loved.

This illustration describes two major defense mechanisms at work: The child denied any wrongdoing or responsibility for her actions and then projected the blame on others when denial was unsuccessful. These defenses usually are present when the uncaring child is faced with anxiety-producing situations.

Because anxiety even in its mild form is painful and unwanted, the uncaring child will maintain and nurture any position necessary to avoid it, even at the expense and emotional cost to her family. If parents have knowledge of the early warning signs of the Uncaring Child Syndrome and have the skills that are necessary when their children are young, there might be more positive outcomes.

Chapter 4:
Early Warning Signs of the
Uncaring Child Syndrome

"Sometimes when I look at my children, I say to myself, Lillian, you should have stayed a virgin."

Mrs. Lillian Carter

Soft Signs

My early attempts to lay the groundwork for a concise manual about the Uncaring Child Syndrome involved lengthy and painstaking explorations into past and present literature dealing with antisocial and conduct disorders. When I had a firm grasp on this body of accumulated knowledge, I began taking a closer look at the early developmental signs of my patients. Were there similarities in their early behaviors that could be understood better? Were there test instruments that I could use that would shed light on these behaviors? Was it possible to objectively describe a sufficient number of behaviors in order to spot this syndrome in its early stage and prevent it?

The following sources give a sampling of several pertinent references to the subject matter along with my review and clinical criteria:

Behavioral Indicators of Delinquent Youngsters

Stanton Samenow (see pages 25-39) described behavioral indicators of delinquent youngsters and listed them as follows:

1. Expecting others to indulge him or her
2. Voracious adventurous appetite
3. Risk-taker
4. Embroiled in difficulties
5. Demanding
6. Projects blame on others
7. Denies wrongdoing
8. Dismisses usual recognition of good deeds
9. Seeks the forbidden
10. Temper tantrums
11. Irresponsible
12. Manipulative

13. Knack for forgetfulness
14. Defiant
15. Poor response to assist with family chores
16. Contempt for advice

Diagnostic Criteria for Antisocial Personality

The Diagnostic and Statistical Manual (DSM IV), published by the American Psychiatric Association in 1994, formulates the diagnostic criteria for the Antisocial Personality Disorder. The following is taken from that source:

"A. There is a pervasive pattern of disregard for and violation of the rights of others occurring since age 15 years, as indicated by three (or more) of the following:

(1) failure to conform to norms with respect to lawful behaviors, as indicated by repeatedly performing acts that are grounds for arrest,

(2) deceitfulness, as indicted by repeated lying, use of aliases, or conning others for personal profit or pleasure,

(3) impulsivity or a failure to plan ahead,

(4) irritability and aggressiveness, as indicated by repeated physical fights or assaults,

(5) reckless disregard for safety of self or others,

(6) consistent irresponsibility, as indicated by repeated failure to sustain consistent work behavior or honor financial obligations, and

(7) lack of remorse, as indicated by being indifferent to or rationalizing having hurt, mistreated, or stolen from another.

B. The individual is at least age 18 years.

C. There is evidence of Conduct Disorder ... with onset before age 15 years.

D. The occurrence of antisocial behavior is not [exclusive] during the course of Schizophrenia or a Manic episode."

Conduct Disorder

In 1994, the American Psychiatric Association released a statement that said, "The essential feature of conduct disorder is a repetitive and persistent pattern of behavior in which the basic rights of others or major age appropriate societal norms or rules are violated." Much controversy exists regarding the lack of distinction between antisocial behavior and conduct behavior. Much of the conduct disorder behavior listed in DSM IV is similar to uncaring behavior.

The major distinction between conduct disorder and uncaring behavior is that uncaring children have a history of uncaring behavior during early childhood. They lack guilt, remorse, and anxiety when those emotions would be expected and appropriate.

The preceding list of behavioral and attitudinal indicators provides us with a realistic understanding that helps to reduce or remove parents' guilt. Parents also feel support in knowing that there are many "good parents" whose children's behavior is not a product of bad parenting. They realize that good parents often have children who show the described behaviors. This list merely supports the evidence that many similarities in unhealthy behavioral patterns exist in children regardless of their being raised by "good" or "bad" parents.

I searched for a more comprehensive understanding of early warning signs that could help parents make strategic and early interventions. My first task was to review all of my files of children with conduct disorders. I then gathered the information of those adolescents with antisocial personality.

Common Problem Behaviors

A review of literature assisted in my quest for understanding and identifying early warning signs. Stanley Turecki, author of *The Difficult Child*, categorized common types of problem behaviors and some parents' descriptions of them:

Types of Behaviors	Parents' Descriptions
Defiant:	• Does what he want to do • Ignores what I say • Does exactly the opposite of what I tell him
Resistive:	• Refuses to listen • Won't follow directions • Dawdles • Always finds excuses
Inattentive:	• Doesn't listen • Tunes out • Daydreams

Types of Behaviors	Parents' Descriptions
Stubborn:	• Has to get his own way • Won't take no for an answer
Shy:	• Very timid • Clings to my skirts • Always hides his or her face
Particular:	• Very picky • Faddish • Wants only certain things • Really hard to please • Fussy, always noticing little things
Complaining:	• Whines a lot • Pouts • Sulks • Never satisfied
Interrupting:	• Interrupts adult conversations • Won't let me talk on the phone
Intrusive:	• Swears a lot • Calls people names
Selfish:	• Takes toys from other children • Rude • Won't share toys • Everything is "mine"
Wild behavior:	• Gets overexcited • Gets revved up easily • Creates a disturbance • Can be destructive
Impulsive:	• Loses control • Has outbursts over little things • Can't seem to stop
Physically aggressive:	• Pushes and shoves people • Hits, kicks or bites other children or even adults
Temper tantrums:	• May vary in intensity and duration

Lynn Weisberg and Rosalie Greenberg (see page 9), authors of *When Acting Out Isn't Acting*, described a problem child as a child with a disruptive disorder. In their experience, disruptive children most often are discovered by the age of seven. "Disruptive classroom behavior at this age makes it increasingly evident that something is wrong."

Literature reveals an increase in the number of problem children. Fortunately, many mental health professionals are beginning to recognize the existence of behavior that is not explained by bad parenting. The information that I gathered was a beginning in determining early warning signs of the Uncaring Child Syndrome. I then compiled data from parents whose children had serious behavioral disorders, utilized test material, and inquired in more detail about the early developmental stages of my patients who were evidencing this syndrome. What follows is a list of those attitudes and behaviors that are most commonly found in my review of children evidencing UCS. The children ranged from four to nineteen years of age. The uncaring child may have only a few or many of the following behaviors:

Attitudes and Behaviors

1. Often lies or makes up stories to get out of trouble
2. Has run away from home overnight or longer
3. Has skipped school
4. Has stolen items or shoplifted
5. Has been suspended or expelled from school
6. Does not listen to parents or teachers
7. Rarely finishes the work that he begins
8. Is easily distracted by noises or people
9. Has difficulty in keeping his mind on schoolwork or other tasks
10. Is impulsive
11. Is a poor organizer
12. Needs constant supervision at home with chores
13. Needs constant supervision at school
14. Cuts up in class
15. Lacks patience
16. Fidgets
17. Disinterested in family or their problems or concerns
18. Has no attachment to personal belongings or to people
19. Is hyperactive

20. Is argumentative
21. Has made threats
22. Has been in trouble with the school, police, or
    a juvenile officer
23. Talks in a superficial manner
24. Engages in moody pondering about abstract matters
25. Fails to learn from experience
26. Lacks guilt or remorse when such a reaction is appropriate
27. Blames or informs on others to avoid punishment
28. Disobeys the rules at home and school
29. Gets upset and displays temper if things don't go
    his or her way
30. Has little or no regard for the rights of others
31. Shows no respect for authority figures
32. Is unreliable
33. Is oppositional
34. Will insist on doing things his or her own way
35. Has sudden mood swings
36. Is easily upset
37. Sees life as a bore and rarely admits to having fun
38. Has poor judgment
39. Has superficial or poor interpersonal relationships
40. Is accident-prone

In my review of the early developmental patterns of these children, I began to see certain similarities that seemed coincidental. Due to their subtle and innocuous nature, these patterns will be referred to as "soft signs."

When one or more of these soft signs persist for more than two weeks, a red flag should go up and we should be alerted to the significance of their meaning. We first must ask, "What is happening in the child's life that can account for such a shift in behavior?" Then, we can ask, "What can we do about it?"

Ken

When I first met fourteen year old Ken, his parents complained of his lying and stealing, which had gotten him in trouble with the police. Ken's parents were unable to end his antisocial criminal behavior and were considering psychiatric hospitalization.

When Ken was four years old, his parents informed me that he refused to listen to them, needed constant supervision, lacked patience, excessively watched television, and showed no attachment to his or anyone's personal belongings. His parents said that Ken had one older brother who was the opposite – "no problem." They began to notice more troublesome behavior when Ken entered the sixth grade. He made failing grades, blamed others to avoid punishment, and lacked guilt whenever confronted about his wrongdoing. The teacher complained that he was a "troublemaker" and made "teaching a chore." He was caught cheating on a test, smoking in the boy's bathroom, and stealing from his classmates. At fourteen, Ken was caught stealing a stereo from a car. It later was learned that he had been involved in this activity for almost a year. Suspicion of neighborhood thefts was directed at him.

Initial attempts to gain Ken's cooperation through individual and family therapy failed. Although he was pleasant and cordial, he could not be believed. At no time did he accept the responsibility for his wrongdoings. He blamed his friends for the thefts by indicating that he was "only holding the stolen articles for them."

Attempts to change the parent's behavior were met with much frustration. Whenever they made some positive headway, Ken would make them believe that he had changed, which produced a breakdown in their progress. Finally, they dropped out of therapy and moved him to a private school.

Ken's story is not uncommon. Parents often feel guilty for acting firm. They want the best for their children and fear that they will do harm if they are perceived as being unfair and inflexible. They fear that their children will leave home, take drugs, and be with undesirable individuals. Ken's parents expressed these ideas throughout their involvement with me. Ken always had been an "operator" and able to manipulate his parents. He created the illusion that he needed to be rescued whenever he got in trouble.

Erica

The parents of Erica, a twenty year old woman, brought her to me after she was caught stealing jeans by a store manager. She had a history of being caught for thefts. Her parents said that she had been a liar since she was nine, was easily upset, rarely learned from experience, had poor judgment, and was impulsive. When she was six, she repeatedly was caught playing with matches. On many occasions, she lost favorite clothing and put objects into the electric sockets to see the sparks. Other soft signs included the lack of guilt and/or remorse when confronted about her wrongdoings and lack of respect for authority figures.

Erica's parents felt that her early behavior was exploratory and told me that her pediatrician said, "She will grow out of it. Just continue to provide her with tender, loving care." She did not grow out of her uncaring behavior; she merely grew into adult antisocial criminal behavior.

After determining that individual and family therapy were ineffective, special parenting techniques were established. Steps were taken to block Erica's uncaring behavior. The parents let her choose to abide by the family rules or leave. They had made these threats many times, but they had not acted on them. Although Erica never changed her behavior, her parent's guilt lessened. Only through a clearer understanding of Erica's early history of uncaring behavior and knowing that they did their very best for her were they able to let go of their anger and guilt. This process was helped by their participation in a parent support group.

We have observed different outcomes of parental action toward uncaring behavior. While Ken's parents chose to allow his behavior to continue by rescuing him and dropping out of therapy, Erica's parents chose to work through the continued difficulties that arose. Erica's parents took charge and did not give in to their anger and guilt.

We must focus on what can be learned from the experience. If parents are able to recognize the soft signs and develop more effective parenting skills, could there be more positive outcomes? Although uncaring children are born with this disorder, it has been my experience that the chances for improvement are substantially enhanced when its existence is recognized in its earliest stage. Improvement does not mean cure. What we can hope to expect from early recognition and identification is the extinction of the undesirable behavior associated with the disorder. For example, the child may never care about the rights of others, feel the emotional pain of others, or experience guilt or remorse for wrongdoings, but the misbehavior associated with these symptoms and behaviors might be changed or removed. Ken's lying, stealing, and failing grades and Erica's stealing and lying might have been extinguished if their parents had been more skilled in the early recognition of soft signs and had adequate skills in parenting the uncaring child.

The following is a list of the earliest soft signs for uncaring children, starting from birth through the age of six years.

Birth – 1 Year
- Has difficulty with play; is easily bored
- Has difficulty in interacting with others
- Resists being held
- Lacks the desire to explore toys

1 – 2 Years
- Is easily distracted by noises or people
- Has sudden mood swings
- Has difficulty in playing competitive games
- Has difficulty in engaging with other children in cooperative play involving group decisions, role assignments, and fair play

2 – 3 Years
- Reacts badly to being told no
- Lacks inquiry or interest in what-and-why questions
- Shows unusual frustration at not being understood
- Lacks even mild anxiety about strangers; is overly ingratiating; responds in the same way to strangers as to familiar people

3 – 4 Years
- Has difficulty in playing by self; does not initiate self-play
- Does not help in putting things away

4 – 5 Years
- Does not ask what-and-why questions
- Lacks the desire for exploration
- Has difficulty with adult directions
- Lacks caring about own possessions
- Is bored when playing in the house

5 – 6 Years
- Lacks concern about what-and-why questions requiring simple answers
- Continues to have difficulty in joining and interacting in play with other children

The following is a list of the characteristic soft signs (red flags) that begin as early as infancy.

Does Not Listen

I repeatedly have heard parents complain that their children don't pay attention to them from as early as two years old. They become preoccupied with television, play, or any number of things. Although frustrated by their children's lack of compliance with rules, parents usually excuse this behavior and attribute it to the age of the child while believing that it will improve in time. The child usually does not return playthings to their proper places, pulls items off of store shelves, goes into the personal belongings of others, and engages in other inappropriate activities.

At the age of two, Debbie often was described as a child who "just didn't listen." She seemed to disregard what was expected or what was said. "She has always had a mind of her own and is very willful," her mother said. "It just doesn't seem to matter how often or what you say to Debbie, she just won't listen."

Is Easily Distracted by Noises or People

This sign has been noted in infancy, but it is more common in children from the age of two. These children are distracted easily and usually have problems with concentration and attention. Although they may be able to concentrate in quiet circumstances, such a child is highly susceptible to interruptions from other stimuli, such as nearby movement and "people noises." If the child is trying to read, work a puzzle, or listen to a story being told, any sudden nearby movement or interference rouses a response that he may not be able to control

Three-year-old Johnny had great difficulty in concentrating. Whenever he was playing, watching television, or being put to bed, he easily was startled by the phone and other noises. His attention would shift to whatever else was happening. His mother said that she noticed this behavior in his crib before he was two years old. "When people came into his room," she said, "he would 'jump out of his skin' as if he saw a ghost."

Lacks Patience

Some children become easily frustrated by their lack of "stick to it-tive-ness." If they are playing with a puzzle and are unable to fit the correct pieces together, they quickly abandon it in favor of another activity. Whenever they face any slight difficulty, this pattern appears. Most importantly, when people behave in this manner repeatedly, it is time to suspect and distrust their motives. We begin to get a picture of how these people deal with conflict and to see their inability to sustain meaningful and healthy human relationships. Few would choose to become friends of these individuals.

Six-year-old Jane was so impatient that she was unable to keep attention on any toy or game for more than a few minutes. Subsequently, she had few friends. The friends that she did have appeared to have the same problems with patience and attention.

Projects Blame

There are other children who find it difficult to accept responsibility for their actions. When their parents or other authority figures confront them, they blame others in order to escape the potential consequences. In a sense, the child is saying, "I'm not the hostile one. It's them."

Victoria was a child who rarely took the blame for anything. If it were not her younger brother's fault, it was her friend's, teacher's, neighbor's, or anyone else's who may have been involved. When she was four years old, she blamed her playmate for ruining her dress. In reality, Victoria spilled ink on it. There were innumerable incidents when she blamed others for her own deeds. When confronted, Victoria rarely admitted her blame. Her parents could remember only a few instances when she took responsibility for her culpability. One example involved accepting the blame for forgetting to inform her father about an important call. Another example concerned her forgetting to feed the dog. In these examples, Victoria did admit to forgetting, but she gave no appearance of genuine concern or emphatic regard for the feelings of her dad or the dog.

Disobeys the Rules at Home and School

In evaluating children who disobey the rules, we can categorize their behavior as mild, moderate, or severe. Obviously, a mild problem affords a better chance for a positive outcome. With more severe disobedience, more effort is required to discourage its continuance.

Estelle's behavior included leaving the lights on throughout the house, leaving the bathroom dirty, failing to lock the doors, not picking up the things in her room, and other infractions. Efforts to correct these behaviors were futile. Reminders and harsh words failed to make things better. By the time that she was eleven, her parents had age-appropriate expectations of Estelle. She, however, did not regard their needs of her as very important. Estelle's behavior was considered to be mild.

Has Little or No Regard for the Rights of Others

By violating the rights of others, people prove how little they respect those rights. Without the capacity of respect, there is little hope of a healthy one on one relationship.

At the age of eight, Michele's continuous "borrowing" of things from her younger sister and mother became a problem. Her lack of concern for their pleas to discontinue this behavior was in vain. There were times when she would use and damage her sister's makeup. Not only would she not tell her about it, she would lie about its use. Many disturbing conflicts arose between the two throughout their relationship at home.

Shows no Respect for Authority Figures

There is a growing concern in this country about the lack of respect for authority figures, including teachers, politicians, and police officers. A growing number of people are becoming more vocal and physically aggressive towards these figures. Society's moral and ethical standards are being undermined. Our children are missing the fundamentals of family values, morals, standards, and goals.

At the age of seventeen, Dennis was taken home by the police. He cursed the policeman for taking the side of his alleged victim. This type of disrespect for authority figures was first noticed when he was nine years old. He mimicked his teachers and parents. His behavior worsened in high school. Much earlier behavior indicated the presence of uncaring signs. When he was four, he was demanding, was stubborn, and had temper outbursts. He displayed little regard for the rights of his playmates and lied.

Has Difficulty with Play

During early childhood, every person develops a need for companionship. Children show a distinct interest in playmates and choose them instead of adults in many instances. These relationships continue throughout the normal development of childhood and adolescence. The soft signs that first appear during early childhood play are in the area of self play and the sharing of toys. Important themes emerge in children at these times. Do they display investigative, imitative, and imaginative play – or are they irritable, crying, and demonstrating temper tantrums? Are they interested or disinterested in other children? Are they competitive and well organized in play while they enjoy peer interaction? They may have destructive tendencies with extreme and uncontrollable uncaring behavior, such as lying, stealing, or intentional cruelty to animals.

By the time that Crystal was four, she already was displaying serious signs of problems at play. While playing with her playmates, she grabbed, tossed, and broke toys. She did not share very well unless she had finished playing with each toy. When agitated by her playmates or with her toys, she would pull out the stuffed animal's arms, eyes, or extremities. Temper outbursts were common.

When Marian was three-and-a-half years old, she enjoyed playing with her stuffed bear. While playing with other children, she could be seen beating up other children's animals with her bear. She refused to allow anyone else to play with it. She seemed interested in playing with the children, but her rough and disturbing play prevented her from receiving successful interactions. There were times when she seemed gentle and caring, but, without warning, roughshod behavior followed.

Is Unreliable

Unreliability is a common and perpetual trait in uncaring children. They rarely can be counted on for any kind of commitment and they make excuses for their lack of following through. When confronted for their failures, uncaring children will quickly divert attention from themselves and leave the confronter dazed, confused, and willing to give the benefit of the doubt to them.

The parents of Marla, a sixteen year old high school student, rarely counted on her. She once agreed to be home in time to supervise her younger brother. Several hours after the arranged time, Marla came home. Her brother had been left unattended. After much confusion and harsh words, Marla blamed her lateness on her boyfriend and the crowds.

Has a Negative Attitude towards School

How children feel about school is significant. Uncaring children often have negative feelings toward teachers and the work that is expected of them. Uncaring children will fix the blame on anyone and make it seem like they are being picked on unfairly. Ironically, they usually look forward to going to school and socializing with their peers, especially children who are very much like them.

Crain always disliked schoolwork. From the time that he was six years old, he rarely did homework because he hated it. His parents said, "He never opens a book to study." Teachers pointed out his tendency to over socialize and his failure to concentrate on studies. Crain's usual complaint was that his teachers were "horrible" and the work that they gave him was excessive.

Superficial or Poor Interpersonal Relationships

Uncaring children are motivated by what they can get. For a time, they may seem highly charged with caring and concern, but they lack staying power. They also do not have the will and drive to follow through. They tend to use their so called friends. However, these friends still may consider them to be their best friends. This may be due largely to their own problems with society in general. Problems in these children's relationships often will emerge when the conflicts become too great for them to handle. They often flee from the discomfort by starting a "new life" in a new setting. In doing so, they reenact their previous unhealthy patterns of behavior that got them into the conflict in the first place.

Tatum was eighteen years old when her world finally fell apart. Her pregnancy and previously strained family relationships made it extremely difficult for her to gain emotional and financial support. Tatum's entire life consisted of lying and manipulation. She rarely, if ever, made attempts to correct the damage or emotional pain that she inflicted on her loved ones. She avoided resolving any of the conflicts that she caused. She showed no remorse or anxiety for her misdeeds nor any concern for those whom she hurt. She usually acted as if she were the victim. Her family and friends were unable to understand her behavior. They spoke of her as "charming and charismatic, yet unreliable, manipulative, and sad." Although she seemed to have no trouble in making male and female friends, they rarely lasted for more than a few months.

Insists on Controlling Things

In spite of many attempts to guide and teach your children, they may resist – stubbornly and dogmatically – while insisting that they already know how to do or handle something. They tend to show contempt for advice. When they mess up, they make excuses or put the blame elsewhere to cover their failure. This type of behavior is frustrating and maddening, but, more significantly, it suggests children with narrow and compulsive mind sets without the concern for knowledge. They also will accept mediocre as their personal standard.

Hal's parents were frustrated by his stubborn personality trait. Regardless of how little he knew, Hal was ready to prove otherwise. Even at the age of six, his parents recalled his refusal to allow them to help in assembling his bike. His stubbornness resulted in some minor damage to the bike. This trait was observed repeatedly when he had difficulty with homework, sports, and some activities around the house. Hal would ignore any advice, hints, or suggestions. He would do it his way in spite of making things more difficult or causing damage.

Has Sudden Mood Swings

Sudden mood swings are observed in children who are extremely sensitive to both external and internal cues. When they perceive a threat from another person, their moods shift so quickly that we usually do not understand the reason for the switch. Sometimes children appear energetic, self confident, and cheerful. They make plans, show interest in activities, and are warm to people. Then, for no apparent reason, their moods shift to depression, anger, sulkiness, or discouragement.

Four-year-old Monica was having fun playing with her doll. When her playmate moved towards her to play, Monica kicked and expressed rage. A few minutes later, Monica was happy and engaged in play with her playmate.

Sees Life as a Bore and Rarely Admits to Having Fun

These kids are difficult to please. They appear to be "burned out" and indifferent to most activities. When they finally appear to be having fun, they do not admit it. They seem to get more satisfaction from acting like the poor victim of society rather than someone who is deriving pleasure from it.

Sara went to Disney World for the day. She pouted and expressed displeasure with the crowds and long lines. While waiting in one line, she complained about wanting to be somewhere else. At the end of the day after riding on almost every attraction, she whined and cried that she missed one ride. She would not let up until her parents expressed frustration and anger. By this time, their day was ruined.

Is Accident-Prone

These children behave a little more daringly than their peers do. They take unnecessary risks and are the proverbial "accident waiting to happen."

Albert continuously hurt himself and broke things. When he was three, he knocked into lamps and broke dishes. By the time that he was twelve, he had broken a finger and a toe, sprained his ankle several times, and fallen off of his bike on several occasions. His parents were reluctant for him to participate in any activity because of their fear for his safety.

Is a Risk-Taker

Risk-takers are known as the ones who seek the forbidden or have voracious appetites for adventure. They appear unafraid and seek out what others avoid.

Ivan was the neighborhood daredevil. He climbed into vacant buildings, dug underground caves, and took risks where others feared to tread. By the time that Ivan was eight years old, he was called "Crazy Ivan." He was afraid of nothing.

Has Run Away from Home Overnight or Longer

Running away from home is more common during the preadolescent and adolescent periods. Continued unresolved problems in the household and at school cause children to flee rather than to solve the dilemma that they have caused. The running away of uncaring children is quite different from that of other children. Uncaring children generally do not have significant amounts of sustained anxiety.

After nine-year-old Tommy was grounded for the week, he failed to come home from school. Later that evening, it was learned that he had gone to his friend's house to spend the night. Tommy lied to his friend's parents about the alleged abuse that he had been receiving from his parents and said that he would like to live with them. After investigating the situation, his parents discovered that Tommy also had lied about his homework and test scores for the past month. They were extremely concerned, so they engaged a therapist to assist them. The parents were considered to be very warm and loving people. Tommy's running away and lying about their alleged abuse was his attempt to make others feel sorry for him. When confronted, he put his head down and said, "I don't know why I lied." This was a typical pattern for his unexplained behavior. While at his friend's home, he displayed none of the expected anxiety and fear until his parents came to pick him up. His apparent fear and anxiety were due to the confrontation "at the moment," not due to the fear of being abused.

Has Skipped School

Skipping school is common among adolescent uncaring children. Because they have disconnected themselves from authority figures and their expectations, the consequences of skipping school are usually of minor concern. Depending upon their uncaring profile (such as that of the chameleon, operator, or any other), they may be quite clever in their deceptions when skipping school or they may show no concern whatsoever for their maladaptive behavior.

Throughout the ninth grade, Jordan cut classes and skipped school entirely. In spite of getting caught on several occasions, his behavior continued. Often he lied about his whereabouts and accused teachers of "having it in" for him. He minimized the importance of the classes that he cut by stating, "I'm getting good grades and felt I could skip class."

Has Stolen Items or Shoplifted

Unlike the normal child, who may steal or shoplift to a very limited extent, uncaring children may derive a sense of pleasure and excitement from the act of stealing. Therefore, they continue their criminal antisocial behavior without regard for its consequence. They may become preoccupied with theft. The very thought of theft is an intense and arousing feeling that they want to repeat. There seems to be a greater sense of pleasure in performing the act itself than in receiving any profit. These children may come from wealthy parents, so the ability to purchase the children's desired objects is not the issue. Chameleons are in the category of uncaring children who more easily can be influenced to steal by their more dominant peers.

Jill, age seventeen, came from an upper-middleclass family. While in therapy, her preoccupation to steal became quite clear. She stated that she got a "high" from the planning of the actual theft. "It was exciting, except getting caught." Throughout her school years, her parents noted that Jill often got involved in behaviors initiated by others. On one occasion, Jill and a few of her friends rode their bikes through a shopping mall for a prank. There were many other such episodes instigated by her more dominant playmates.

Has Been Suspended or Expelled From School

The lack of respect for authority and the lack of concern for the consequences of their misbehavior often lead these children to face the possibility of suspension and, on rare occasions, expulsion from school. Because of truancy, talking back to teachers, fighting, or disrupting their environment, these children are more likely to become suspended.

By the age of seventeen, Joey already had been suspended six times. The reasons included talking back to teachers, fighting, and disruptive behavior in class and on the school grounds. On each occurrence, he blamed the teacher or the students for his actions. He never looked at his own behavior as the possible cause.

Has Made Threats

Threatening the wellbeing of others is certainly more serious behavior than skipping school. When behavior reaches this level, it must be stopped. Besides being a clear and present danger to the safety and wellbeing of others, this behavior also could be harmful to the child.

At the age of fourteen, Pam was suspended for fighting in school. When she got home, she told her mother that she was going to kill the other girl for getting her into trouble. On two other occasions, Pam made threats towards others who had offended her. Although the rage eventually diminished, Pam was unwilling and unable to appreciate her role in making the problems worse.

Has Been In Trouble with the School, Police, or Juvenile Officer

This type of behavior is exhibited by not doing homework, being disrespectful, fighting, talking back, stealing, using drugs and alcohol, making threats, and acting in other harmful ways. A persistent and blatant pattern of uncaring behaviors usually is associated with the act. If children wind up with the juvenile authority of a police department, for example, you can be fairly certain that a pattern of uncaring behaviors existed prior to their current dilemmas. Additionally, these children are usually in conflict with their parents.

The police stopped Mason for speeding. He became unruly and rude to the police officer when questioned about his suspended driver's license. As a result of his behavior, he was taken to the police station. It was learned that he had three additional speeding tickets and four moving violations in the past year and a half. His parents indicated that he had a history of foul language, disrespectfulness, and problems at school.

Speaks Superficially

Talking superficially is a way of avoiding basic issues. Instead of discussing important concerns, children may spend a great deal of time talking about the topics of the day, their friends, or their past experiences. There is little significance in what they are saying and they may go on talking about anything that has little bearing on the problems at hand.

Since the age of eight, Jane seemed to talk around issues. She could never be pinned down to any particular topic. For example, when she failed to clean her room, she stated that she would "get to it" and then discussed her broken stereo, her friend's new dog, and other unrelated thoughts. Her parents remarked about how difficult and frustrating it was to deal with any single issue. When it came to discussing her progress in school, her talk focused on circumstantial and unrelated issues about her improved performance since the last report card, "bad teachers, rotten school," clothing, vacations, and other invalid justifications.

Expects Indulgence from Others

Some children put little of themselves into relationships. They are takers, not givers. They expect parents to provide clothing in the latest styles, give undeserved spending money, and present special gifts to them on a regular basis. When they are asked to help with chores, they act indignant or claim to be too busy.

Lana was a child who expected her parents to provide the latest clothes and spending money. When she was sixteen, she expected a new car and money to buy insurance. There rarely was a time when her parents could depend on her for anything. She could be found sitting on the couch, watching television, and going to the refrigerator. When the family was working on chores or other projects, she left the house. All of the people who were close to her considered her to be lazy.

Dismisses Usual Recognition of Good Deeds

Although these children are given recognition for good deeds and are treated with special rewards, they have a need to demonstrate their misery by avoiding feelings of success. This is largely due to poor self esteem and an intolerable sense of failure. When they do accept recognition for their good deeds, they quickly seize upon the opportunity to gain a manipulative foothold.

When Bobbie's parents told her how wonderfully she did on her tests, she asked for fifteen dollars and permission to borrow their car. Whenever her parents praised her, they felt that she would take that opportunity to get something in return from them. "She never just said thanks." She rarely looked pleased at the praise and responded by pouting or with anger. It was their feeling that Bobbie did not wish to be expected to complete anything, so her response was usually contrary.

Is Manipulative

When attempts of deceiving other people are successful, they are sources of satisfaction for uncaring children. When they are not, these children may display contempt or make other demands until they are successful. They feel that they deserve what they are attempting to gain and experience no guilt for their actions. Because they feel deprived and victimized, they are able to rationalize their manipulative activities as being appropriate.

Joshua became angry and gloomy when his father didn't let him use the car. Continuing his efforts to make his father feel guilty, Joshua told his therapist that he usually was successful in making his parents do what he wanted them to do. Even though they felt that they were being used, they continued to give in to his needs. They rationalized that, "Josh wasn't much different than most other sixteen-year-old boys. After all, he wasn't doing drugs."

Has Knack for Forgetfulness

When a parent asks a child, "Why haven't you done your home-work?" or "Why haven't you taken out the trash?" he or she replies, "I forgot." This is probably the most common complaint that I hear from parents when they describe areas of frustration with their children. We jokingly begin to wonder if there is a cognitive hearing-deficit epidemic that is being transmitted throughout the country. There is sometimes no distinction between the forgetfulness of the normal child and that of the uncaring child.

Denise agreed to clean her room each week on Sunday. Unless her parents reminded her, she failed to perform this task half of the time.

Receives Poor School Grades

One of the most useful soft signs, especially for pre adolescents and adolescents, that can serve as a red flag of concern is declining school grades. This is measurable behavior that cannot be disputed. Many times, children will insist that their poor grades are errors made by their teachers or are the results of child/teacher conflicts. Then, they promise to do better. This is when parents should take special notice. Poor grades should serve as a reference point that may indicate the need to look more deeply into their children's situations.

Melinda's first problem with school grades occurred in the fourth grade. When she reached middle school, her grades had dropped to C's and D's. Whenever her parents approached her regarding her progress, she replied, "I'm doing better this semester." There was rarely a time when Melinda accepted the responsibility for her sub-average performance.

For the purpose of early prevention and treatment of children who may be exhibiting the Uncaring Child Syndrome, the early warning signs (soft signs or red flags) are offered for consideration. There are many varieties of and similarities among the maladaptive behavioral patterns of uncaring children. When we are better informed, we are better prepared to deal more effectively. Until now, uncaring children have had the upper hand. They have been in control and have played havoc with the family structure. Parents have lost power and their ability to parent. Without a complete understanding of the Uncaring Child Syndrome, most parents remain defenseless and ill equipped to neutralize their children's destructive nature. The recognition of early warning signs adds to the parents' skills. Fortification of the family's position is made possible by this knowledge. Parents clearly can identify misbehavior by the early recognition of soft signs. When they are properly identified, early intervention can be affected. With early intervention, there is a greater opportunity for changing unhealthy patterns of behavior. When the misbehavior exists for longer and longer periods of time, it becomes increasingly more difficult to change.

Chapter 5:
Follow the Leader

"There are times when parenthood seems like nothing but feeding the mouth that bites you."
Peter De Oris

Peer pressure, television, celebrities, religious leaders, and politicians are all credited as major influences in swaying public opinion. Although we recognize our ability to sort out information and make informed choices, it is impressive how certain people have the ability to influence others. Uncaring and even antisocial individuals occupy some of the highest offices in the government of the United States. How often do we read or hear about prominent figures accused and sometimes convicted of cold and shameless crimes unbefitting and incongruent to what we expected from them?

Some children follow the misguided suggestions of particular playmates who lead them into trouble. In spite of otherwise-good judgment, they mindlessly follow a strong suggestion. When uncaring children follow the lead of more dominant uncaring others, this combination of dangerous elements can lead to tragic consequences.

Have you ever noticed how some individuals seem to have the unusual ability of gaining attention and influencing others? They have that certain unexplained quality called charisma, charm, or power. Other people seem to follow their lead as if they were hypnotized.

Power and dominance are the focus of this chapter because they may hold the key that unlocks the mysteries of unexplained behaviors, especially those behaviors that seem unmotivated, without direction, or even dangerous.

Many scientific studies by Thorleif Schjelderupp-Ebbe, a Norwegian zoologist, compare human and animal behavior. Unfortunately, the observations and conclusions from these studies have yet to be put into full use. When we observe the behavior of chickens, we note the presence of the "pecking order." A hierarchy of dominance and power is obvious in the group. The chickens with the most power peck the ones with the least power. We see the same phenomenon in most species of animals.

Abraham Maslow, a psychologist who is famous for his theory of the hierarchy of needs, examined relationships among monkeys in 1936. He saw that the monkeys were preoccupied with sex and that they did not discriminate between the sexes. Male monkeys mounted other males and females mounted other females. Of course, both sexes also mounted the opposite sex. Maslow concluded that the highly dominant apes mounted the less dominant ones, regardless of gender.

In 1979, dominant and subdominant behavior in the animal kingdom also was documented in the work of Diane Fossey, who fought to save the African mountain gorilla from extinction. During the 1980's, the naturalist Jane Goodall studied this dominance while observing apes in Africa.

The Korean War produced an amazing yet similar discovery regarding humans. During the war, not one American ever escaped from Korean captors. The Koreans were able to pick out those prisoners whom they felt were dominant and place them in quarters that were separate from their subdominant peers. When the subdominant prisoners were not under the influence of the dominant ones, they were easy to control (See "Kinkead" on pages 128-130).

The Korean captors were able to understand their influence on the prisoners. When the indoctrination program began, these men were isolated, sent to separate camps, and given hard labor details.

In the Wang Report, another account described the basic communist techniques used on American soldiers in China and in Korea (See "Kinkead" on pages 128-130). Of significant importance in this report was the ability of the captors to identify the least resistive candidates for indoctrination. They found that the most cooperative were the young enlisted men of higher socioeconomic status.

The significance of this finding is the idea of influencing the young. The example of Korean indoctrination may help us to understand more clearly the susceptibility of our youth in following the destructive antisocial signals of their peers and society.

Why is this dominant theory so vitally important in the field of human development, especially when dealing with children's behavior? How can we best use this information when faced with our children's disruptive behavior at home or at school?

The answers are as fascinating as the questions. First, let us return to the earlier comparison of humans to other forms in the animal kingdom. When we are forced to live in confined quarters, such as in jails or ghettos, we behave much like Maslow's monkeys in the Bronx Zoo. Confinement can cause increases in domestic violence, sexual activity, frustration, and gang participation. Children, like monkeys, occupy positions on the dominance scale and they remain on their respective levels due to peer pressure. Like actors in a Shakespearean play, they remain true to their roles. They take on the characteristics and mannerisms that are dictated by the more dominant personalities in their social groups. Their roles become strengthened and reinforced by the positive acknowledgments of their groups. Without realizing it, they become mindless, brainwashed, or programmed members of a common group process.

Jim Jones

The phenomenon that is mentioned above was prevalent in the followers of Jim Jones. Jones was the preacher who led hundreds of his sect to commit mass suicide in Guyana. On November 18, 1978, the hideous tragedy occurred. The mass murders and suicides at Jonestown, the name of Jim Jones, and the People's Temple will never fade from most of our memories because an incident of frightful and catastrophic proportion took place.

When I first heard of that catastrophe, I wondered how one person could easily influence so many people. It was difficult to comprehend how individuals from many diverse walks of life could surrender themselves to the yearnings of Jim Jones. My first reaction to the slaughter was to suppose that these individuals did not have strong wills of their own and were rejects of society. I later learned that this was not the case. There was a diversity of class, intellect, skills, and wealth within the membership of the cult. Thoughts continued to plague me regarding the submission of so many people to one leader, one voice, and one command. What possibly could make individuals obey such destructive demands in such a mindless and dangerous fashion? What were the forces at play that could explain this phenomenon?

We were compelled to acknowledge the fact that people from all walks of life can be programmed and dominated to perform the most horrifying and repulsive acts of violence on others and themselves. Here was a religious leader, whose previous behavior had demonstrated a love for humanity and love for humankind, who turned his humility and love into antisocial criminal brutality.

Charles Manson

Another case is that of Charles Manson, the leader of a cult in southern California and the man who was convicted of masterminding several brutal murders. In each instance, a clearly defined dominant leader subjugated the less dominant followers.

Having studiously followed the Manson saga, I was intrigued by the dominance and control that he held over his followers. I first heard about the Manson murders in 1970, but it wasn't until 1974 (when *Helter Skelter* by Vincent Bugliosi was first published) that I became interested in the issues related to domination. This book deeply explored a person who had the power to direct his evil thoughts at those under his influence. Mindlessly and without hesitation, his followers would commit some of the most ruthless criminal acts in American history.

Helter Skelter offers an unusual glance into the dark mind of Charles Manson. The book's author states that Manson believed that "Fear is beneficial... Fear is the catalyst of action. It is the energizer, the weapon built into the game in the beginning, enabling a being to create an effect upon himself, to spur himself on to new heights and to brush aside the bitterness of failure."

Manson needed to be around weak people whom he could use. He would repeat phrases in order to program them while instilling fear. He made them believe that the Manson family members were the only ones who cared about each other. He was described as having charisma and an incredibly persuasive power. He had strong beliefs that followed Friedrich Nietzsche's philosophy, which, according to Bugliosi, says, "Women are inferior to men; the white race is superior to all the other races; it is not wrong to kill if the end is right."

Manson was a person who also knew how to convince his followers that he had magical powers. His con-man techniques were effective in supplying what they needed. Drugs were used as an effective agent to make his followers more compliant and obedient to his commands. According to Bugliosi, Manson once said, "You can convince anybody of anything if you just push it at them all of the time. They may not believe it 100 percent, but they will still draw opinions from it, especially if they have no other information to draw their opinions from."

Manson became the only source of information for his followers. He managed to create an environment that totally conformed to his reality. He created a family that loved and cared for each other – and killed for him!

Charles Lindholm, professor and author, said, "...the group obeys certain natural tendencies; however, these tendencies were not toward spontaneous creation, but toward mindless repetition."

The relationship between Manson and his followers, as well as that between Jim Jones and his followers, is the strangest and most important aspect of the dominant-versus-subdominant theme. It is this relationship, this merger of two different forces, that can generate the spark that creates either pointless brutality or beneficial and constructive deeds. Both Jones and Manson represent the negative forces of destruction, but positive and constructive relationships that produce healthy outcomes do exist. Teachers, religious leaders, parents, therapists, politicians, and others lead and help our children. In many cases, it is difficult to determine which advice is good or bad. How are we to know what leaders are good or bad – or will turn bad if given too much power? What is too much power? The peculiar relationship between a highly dominant person and his subordinates can produce various concerns. What are the factors that enable one person to have power over another? How do these individuals meet? What are the conditions that cause a person to act out aggressive and destructive tendencies? I raise these questions in order to look more closely at the workings of the dominant and subdominant mind.

Robert Ardrey, the American author of African Genesis, stated, "In any group of eight or ten, random chance would dictate that one at least had superior capacities." He went on to say, "So it may be that what seems [to be an] insanely small group of a dozen or twenty or a hundred individuals may with the desperate dedication seek to force on all human populations [the] acceptance of the group's illusion."

Characteristics of High Dominance

The characteristics of the highly dominant individual are as follows:

1. has little regard for what people think of him

2. has temper outbursts
3. is aggressive
4. is stubborn
5. is highly motivated to achieve personal goals
6. has no respect for others
7. thinks that honesty is a lesser value
8. has many friends but is easily disliked
9. has charm and charisma to attract others to follow
10. lacks sensitivity and regard for the rights or feelings of others
11. has firm and unbending beliefs
12. is a skillful manipulator
13. lacks guilt, shame, or remorse
14. is arrogant
15. is highly persuasive
16. is a thrill seeker
17. is extremely intuitive in knowing what people want

Lindholm discusses the presence of a "central and inspiring figure to rouse them [the dominated] to action; a stone needs to be thrown, the organizing gesture made." In 1903, Gabriel Tarde, a social psychologist who conceived sociology as based on small psychological interactions among individuals, wrote, "Human beings are portrayed as unconscious puppets who mechanically imitate whatever arouses them from their torpor [stupor]." Sigmund Freud, the father of psychoanalysis, feared the charismatic leaders and the power that they could wield over the populous, Kinkead (1959).

What we have learned thus far is two fold: First, there are those who have special inborn abilities to control others and, second, there are those who can be controlled. The most useful knowledge for parents to learn from this chapter is the information that clearly identifies the characteristics and personality traits of the dominant versus the sub-dominant types. I don't believe that having special knowledge of these traits can have much bearing on changing them, but it might help to identify, recognize, and prevent tragedies from occurring.

For example, your eight year old boy is playing with several youth in the neighborhood. Spotting the dominant traits of one of his play-mates, you become more alert and cautious in allowing your son to continue this relationship. This would be true especially if your son has a subdominant personality. The comparison of dominant to subdominant characteristics presented later in this chapter will help you to spot and identify your children's traits. It also can be beneficial in helping to prevent possible harm. Like asthmatic or hearing-impaired children, subdominant children are like preys of lions. They are and always may be at risk.

Paul

Paul was seventeen when he was brought to my attention. His parents told me that he was a dutiful young boy throughout his childhood. He was especially close to his mother and spent a great deal of time with her when his father was at work. His parents said, "Paul was a good boy, sensitive and sweet."

When he was sixteen, he met Trish, a girl who was his senior by three years. He fell deeply and madly in love. Initially, his parents offered no resistance to his first love, but they soon began to sense their son's personality change. He became argumentative, demanding, and hostile. As the relationship intensified, Paul leveled attacks on his mother by stating that she was "phony and stupid."

After meeting this family in therapy, I was convinced that Paul's complaints were unfounded and irrational. When asked about his accusations about his mother, he would repeat the same phrase, "She's a fake and a phony," or he would say, "She's sick," or "She's stupid." When I pressed him to expand on his statements, he brought up vague references to his early childhood. He said that his mother touched his penis when he was about three years old. He also recalled how his mother embarrassed him by kissing him in front of his friends when he was fifteen years of age. Other than these complaints, Paul was unable to elaborate on any reasons why he was so greatly disturbed at this time in his life. His only wish was to leave his parents' home, live with his girlfriend, and yet continue to be supported by his parents until he was fully independent.

When I met Paul's girlfriend, Trish, I was impressed by the energy that she radiated while attempting to convince me that Paul needed to leave his parents. She described the problems that he was having with his parents and his need to "break away from their grasp." She indicated that they were "overbearing" and they "used him." She emphasized that they rarely had paid any attention to him while he was growing up and spent all of their time either with their business or traveling. She described Paul as coming from deviant parents who never loved him. She further stated that his mother was "sick" because "she smothered him, keeping him from growing up."

Because of the complexity of this rapidly disintegrating situation, I called for a family meeting. As I spoke with Paul's twenty year old brother and fourteen year old sister, I was impressed by their concern for Paul and their warmth for their parents. They were articulate and gave me the impression that Paul, although a sensitive and caring boy, spent a great deal of time alone in his room and did not have many friends. As a child, he gave toys, money, or any other personal belongings to his friends in order to keep their friendship. His siblings also indicated that Paul "worshiped" his mother and, until he fell in love with Trish, they were inseparable. He was very dependent on his mother for making appointments, planning schedules, helping with homework, and assisting with many other activities. He needed an inordinate amount of reassurance and praise. He always was concerned about what people thought about him. He feared that he was disliked and that he would never have friends.

What is most beneficial about reading Paul's story is the understanding that it brings regarding subdominant personality characteristics. Paul never seemed to have an identity of his own. His personality appeared to be part of another person's personality, which is much like the chameleon in Chapter 2. In other words, Paul needed others in order to feel whole. During his early life, he shared his personality with his mother. His over-dependence on her, his need for approval, and her unintentional support of this detrimental development inhibited his healthy emotional growth.

He was clearly a subdominant young man who was later lured by a woman's dominant influence. Trish was able to convince Paul that his parents were "bad" and she was "good." Paul was madly in love and in lust with her, so he was very much afraid of losing her if he did not leave his parents. She presented herself as the only one who truly understood him, loved him, and could help to free him of his "bad" parents. Paul seemed helplessly and hopelessly dominated, but felt a great deal of power as long as he did his girlfriend's bidding. Extremely important during the initial phase of Paul's relationship with Trish was his attempt to commit suicide when she threatened to leave him. Paul told me that she was leaving because of an argument that they had about her considering going back to her previous boyfriend. Additionally, she was angry about his continuing to live with his parents.

Shortly after Paul moved in with Trish, he dropped out of therapy. Paul's parents were left with a feeling of guilt and sorrow. Although they were able to reestablish a relationship with him, he would never visit them without having Trish present and, even then, the contact was brief. Paul continued to accept financial support for car payments, insurance, and other living expenses. His parents felt that they would lose him completely if they discontinued their support.

Linda

Linda was eight years old when she began to demonstrate serious problems at school. Her teachers told her parents that she was "bossy, stubborn, aggressive, and creating disturbances in the classroom." One teacher told them about an incident during which Linda persuaded two of her classmates to play a trick on another girl. This prank resulted in the breakage of the victim's birthday watch. The teacher indicated that this was not the first such incident that Linda had orchestrated.

Linda's parents said that she was a strong-willed young girl who had been difficult to rear. She always argued with her siblings. They said that she always "had" to be right. In spite of her aggressiveness with her peers, she had friends.

What was being disclosed was the profile of a dominant and possibly uncaring girl. She was relatively indifferent to what people said or felt about her behavior. She showed little regard for the rights of others. She had highly adapted manipulative skills and she had a certain charismatic charm with her peers. From all reports, Linda had to be the boss.

When dominant and subdominant people get together, there is always the possibility of a lethal interaction. If the dominant happens to be an uncaring individual, it is easy to imagine the potential for disaster. Combining the uncaring dominant and the subdominant can produce great harm.

I have compiled my findings about dominance in uncaring children and have listed them in the following table. These personality traits will help you to detect the differences between dominant characteristics and subdominant characteristics. This comparative material is taken from over four decades of my clinical experience, data collection, case material, resource literature, clinical profiles, and personal investigation.

Comparisons of
Dominant and Subdominant Children

Dominant Uncaring Children	Subdominant Children
Usually take the responsibility of making the decisions	Rarely assume the responsibility of making decisions
Have little regard for what people think about them	Are very much concerned about what others feel or think about them
Have temper outbursts when they do not get their way	Usually yields to the more dominant
Are likely to be more aggressive	Are likely to be less aggressive
Are stubborn	Are usually agreeable
Are highly motivated to achieve personal goals	Are poorly motivated towards goal achievement
Rarely show anxiety	Often exhibit anxiety
Are very selective in giving others respect	Are very envious and often give respect to others
Are highly sexual and feel free to experiment sexually	Have little desire for sex except for procreation

Dominant Uncaring Children	Subdominant Children
Feel that honesty is a lesser value	Feel that honesty is important; easily manipulated to be dishonest when under control of a dominant person
May have many friends, but are disliked easily	Have few friends and often are not liked
Usually prefer to be alone, but will be with others as long as the others follow their lead	Usually prefer to be with others
Lack sensitivity, empathy, warmth and regard for the feelings of others	Are very sensitive to how others feel
Have firm and inflexible beliefs	Have loose and flexible beliefs
Are very demanding	Are not very demanding
Are skilled manipulators	Are easily manipulated
Lack the usual guilt and remorse for wrongdoings	Experience undue guilt and remorse for perceived wrongdoings
Have the charm and charisma to attract others	Lack the ability to attract others
Tend to be arrogant	Tend to be humble
Are very perceptive and intuitive in knowing what people want	Are very sensitive to giving what other people want and need
Are highly persuasive	Are easily persuaded
Are thrill seekers	Avoid thrill seeking unless in the control of a more dominant individual

Chapter 6:
Alcohol, Drugs, and Crime

"Here's to alcohol: the cause of, and answer to, all of life's problems."

Matt Groening
American cartoonist and creator of "The Simpsons,"
the animated television program

The purpose of this chapter is the distinguishing of drug and alcohol behavior from the behavior of the uncaring child. Is an adolescent's abuse of drugs or alcohol an early warning sign of uncaring and/or antisocial criminal behavior or is it merely an illness associated with substance abuse? This chapter explores the immense drug and alcohol abuse problem as well as the moral and social problems resulting from our children's indulgence and abuse.

First, let us look at the effects that drug and alcohol abuse have on the child and society. The typical user/abuser consumes drugs to get high, which feels good. Since drugs are everywhere, a child has no difficulty in obtaining them. Alcohol, marijuana, cocaine, and crack are the most popular and the easiest drugs to acquire. Many of the children answer yes to the question, "Do you know anyone in your school or neighborhood who has used or is selling drugs?"

The general consensus today is that anyone can be addicted. There is no personality type for the alcoholic or drug abuser. There is evidence, however, that a person has a greater chance of becoming addicted to alcohol and drugs if one or both parents are alcoholics.

The most widely abused drug today is alcohol. That is probably due to its legality. Many of the kids who abuse alcohol also are using other chemicals. These at risk children show signs of emotional problems, such as anger, rage, depression, and psychosis. I often have heard teenagers say that they believe marijuana is harmless. They insist that there is no conclusive evidence to prove that it is dangerous. In fact, they believe that it is much less dangerous than alcohol. My observations paint a different picture. I have found that children who are using marijuana often fit into the category of those who have lost interest and motivation in their schoolwork and in their relationships with their parents. One of my sixteen-year-old patients, a marijuana user, said to me, "If you think me or my friends are going to contribute to anything positive to this world, then think again." Prior to his drug usage, his parents told me, "He was a good boy who was very affectionate." Unfortunately, due to his continual use of drugs, it was impossible to reach any of his positive traits. The drugs had taken over his thinking and attitude.

Of course, there is the inherent danger of driving while drinking or drugging. The danger to oneself and others becomes obvious. Sadly, the abuser's judgment and insight into the potential danger is grossly impaired. In addition, of course, it is illegal to use these drugs. The resultant cost to personal property and life is enormous.

The effect that intoxication has on uncaring individuals is the lowering of their resistances to criminal impulses. While intoxicated, they are less likely to care about the rights of others or the dangerous outcomes of their behaviors. Even in everyday "normal" conflicts, the uncaring personality can be lethal. The uncaring and unloving person who lacks good judgment and guilt can become harmful and dangerous with the addition of alcohol or drugs.

Let us suppose that an uncaring boy's girlfriend leaves him. Intoxicants intensify his anger and rage. Alcohol and drugs reduce his ability to control his impulses to do harm. With an already-impaired ability to use good judgment, he acts on his impulse to do harm without any consideration of the consequences. This lethal combination of intoxicants and uncaring traits gives rise to his criminal attitude and behavior.

How does the uncaring and drinking/drugging combination differ from that of a caring child who drinks or drugs? Although many criminal types use intoxicants, most drinkers/druggers are not criminals and not all alcohol-related crimes are committed by antisocial criminals. In the next three examples, we see how chemicals can affect different personality types.

Mitchell

Because alcohol addiction creates a powerful hold on the abuser, this hold must be broken prior to any attempt to treat uncaring behavior.

Mitchell was eighteen years old when he was arrested for burglary and grand theft for the fifth time. At the time of his arrest, he was intoxicated by alcohol and other chemicals. Although the intoxicants could be blamed for reducing his judgment, thereby leading to the commission of the crimes, they could not be the cause of his repeated criminal activity. His drinking/drugging behavior was an extension of his criminal pursuits. Like most individuals who use and abuse substances, Mitchell used alcohol and drugs for the purposes of seeking pleasure, relieving tension, reducing stress, cheering bad moods, and helping with sleep. He felt more sociable, sexy, and outgoing when under the influence. Sadly, due to his criminal antisocial personality, Mitchell's involvement in drug and alcohol abuse contributed to the increase of his criminal impulses. His continued use of these substances helped to maintain and even increase his antisocial criminal activities.

Lawrence

Lawrence's story is a good illustration of the difference between the uncaring individual and the alcoholic. Lawrence was eighteen years old when he was arrested for drunk driving. He had no other criminal record. His drinking problem began when he was thirteen years old. It caused many hardships for his family and friends. Yet, during the entire course of his problem with alcohol, he was never involved in any illegal behavior. In fact, his guilt and remorse were quite apparent after every drinking episode. Everyone who knew Lawrence spoke of him in glowing but sad terms. They said that he was caring, sensitive, and loving when he abstained from alcohol. The picture of the alcoholic is confusing sometimes. His anger, lies, unreliability, personality, and mood swings are not much different from those of the uncaring child. The major difference is in his capacity for guilt and remorse after he has had too much to drink. Uncaring people often show no concern for the serious harm that they cause to themselves or others. On the other hand, alcoholics like Lawrence do not have a history of uncaring behavior (such as skipping school, rebelling against authority, and running away) prior to their alcohol abuse.

Typical alcoholics respond better to treatment than alcoholic uncaring individuals do. I must emphasize that alcoholics can cause the same amount of devastation to their families, friends, relatives, and society as that caused by uncaring individuals or antisocial criminals. This is largely due to the extent of the crime that is committed. It is certainly fair to say that typical alcoholics under the influence of intoxicants can rob, steal, and even kill. Although alcohol or drug abuse does not change people into antisocial criminals, it is quite possible for people who are under the influence to commit antisocial criminal acts.

It is difficult enough to deal with uncaring children without the influence of intoxicants. With the added problem of use/abuse, the treatment of the uncaring child becomes a nightmare.

I recall a single parent and his girlfriend who came to me for advice. His nineteen-year-old son had a history of lying, stealing, disrespecting authority, lacking motivation, being truant, and failing courses. During the two years prior to our association, he became addicted to alcohol and marijuana. The father wanted me to help him to stop his son's misbehavior and marijuana use, but he felt that it was "normal" for his son to continue drinking because drinking was socially acceptable.

The addictive areas must be dealt with first when treating this condition. Addiction to alcohol and drugs must be eliminated in order for the uncaring behaviors to be addressed. It would be like treating a suicidal spouse for marital problems before first securing the person's safety. Working on marital issues would be useless if the person committed suicide. Likewise, working on uncaring behavior is useless when drinking/drugging continues.

Crack, a highly additive drug, has wrecked havoc on kids throughout the United States. Crack is a purified and extremely addictive form of cocaine. Its low price, widespread availability, immediate effect, and intense gratification make it highly desirable. Most drug abuse specialists agree that, once you use it, it uses you.

Mark

Mark came from a hard-working middleclass family. Other than exhibiting moderate hyperactivity and a reading problem, he and his parents got through his early years and schooling without a great deal of difficulty. Mark was very intelligent and had mechanical talents. He followed his father's example and headed toward a career in the plumbing field. He had been working beside his father for almost a year when he explored crack for the first time. Within a few days, Mark was lying and argumentative. After a month, he began to steal from his parents and pawn their personal belongings. His personality began to change rapidly. He made excuses for not going to work. His hostility turned into rage. Only when Mark came home early one morning and was bloodstained did his parents know that he was in serious trouble. Mark said that he was in a car accident after leaving his girlfriend's house. They later discovered that he was lying. They began to find drug paraphernalia, such as pipes, baggies, rolling paper, and seeds. A medical examination revealed high blood pressure, rapid pulse rate, and dehydration. A blood test for drug screening was performed with positive results. He admitted to using marijuana, alcohol, and crack. He agreed to go to counseling.

The counseling efforts that followed were extremely painful and almost tragic. Mark had six backslides during the first six months of treatment. For the first month, I saw him twice each week. After several relapses, he agreed to enter a drug rehabilitation program for one month. During that period and the months that followed, Mark continued to have short episodes when he used coke and crack. After his parents had reported him missing for three days, he was found severely beaten. When he was admitted to the hospital's emergency room, his physical condition was so deteriorated that they barely could keep him alive. During the months that followed, Mark and his parents endured a great deal of worry, frustration, financial decay, and anger. Fortunately, the outcome was positive. He went back to school and eventually earned his contractor's license. Even then, Mark's abuse of crack and cocaine continued to haunt him. He still had the desire to use crack. He fought the powerful effects of the drug's addictive qualities every single day. He indicated that he could smell and taste crack even though he had not used it for over a year. On several occasions, crack addicts have reported this smell and taste phenomenon to me.

Although Mark could not be classified as an uncaring child, his drug-related behavior was similar. He lied, stole, and had little regard for the rights and feelings of others. One thing was different: He experienced and expressed an enormous amount of guilt and shame. Unfortunately, when the need arose, he sought out the source of the drug without regard for those whom he loved the most and those who most loved him. He would lie, steal, borrow, beg, and humiliate himself for his narcotics.

He stole jewelry that was given to his mother by her mother in Russia. Although he was aware of the tremendous sentimental value that it held for her, he took it, anyway. Mark indicated that he had no control over his addiction or what he might do to get the drug.

I now will clarify the differences between the uncaring drinker/drugger and the treatable drinker/drugger. There are significant differences between the uncaring drinking/drugging profile and the treatable drinking/drugging profile. These differences are:

Drinking/Drugging Profile

Uncaring Drinker/Drugger	Treatable Drinker/Drugger
History of misbehavior usually prior to the alcohol/drug abuse (lying, stealing, truancy, conflicts with authority, police, running away, and the like	Uncaring behavior follows drug and alcohol use; criminal actions occur under the influence of drugs or alcohol
Lack of guilt, remorse, or shame for their uncaring acts	Shows guilt, remorse, or shame for his uncaring actions
Use of drugs and alcohol did not cause his uncaring misbehavior	Drug and alcohol abuse may cause his uncaring acts
Difficulty in establishing a career	Predictability in establishing a career
Early onset of drug and alcohol use/abuse	Early or later onset of drug and alcohol use/abuse
Drug and alcohol intake is more likely to be associated with criminal behavior	Drug and alcohol intake is less likely to be associated with criminal behavior
Impulsiveness	Some impulsiveness
Lack of good judgment and insight	Some lapses of good judgment and insight

Uncaring Drinker/Drugger	Treatable Drinker/Drugger
Problems with work and personal life	Minor problems with work and personal life
Likely to abuse spouse and family with or without the intake of chemicals	Slight chances of abusing spouse and family with or without the intake of chemicals

The effects of drug and alcohol abuse do not reach only those who have the choice to explore their evil offering. There are those who are born into its ever-reaching grip. Everyday, infants are born with either an addiction or with a propensity toward behavior that makes normal child development difficult.

Sean

Sean was a sixteen year old teenager whose use and abuse of drugs had been going on for at least a year. From his early childhood, he was described as aggressive and demanding. When he was caught lying and stealing, he would blame others for his deeds. He had little regard for the rights and welfare of others. He rarely, if ever, showed guilt or remorse for what he had done.

By the time that Sean was in high school, he was the leader of a gang of his peers. They were known to use drugs, bully and extort money from other schoolchildren, and create a disturbance to everyone. During the course of his first two years in high school, Sean and his pals served internal and external suspensions. His parents were called to school on numerous occasions. They admitted that they had little control over his attitude and behavior.

On one occasion, Sean was placed in a thirty day drug rehabilitation facility. He was considered to be a model client and was released to his parents. Within two weeks, he resumed his antisocial behavior. Individual psychotherapy and family counseling also were attempted with no success.

A school counselor referred Sean to me. He informed me that Sean's parents and the school were unable to stop his destructive behavior.

They assigned him to an alternative classroom, but his negative influence reached out to others whom he led into further disruptions.

I reviewed Sean's early childhood conduct, his parents' attitudes, their involvement with him, and his response to therapy and drug rehabilitation. A pattern of uncaring behavior evolved. At the age of two, Sean had temper outbursts and was demanding, impulsive, defiant, and selfish. By the time that he was eight, he was known as a bully, a liar, an "antagonizer," and one who could lead his peers to misbehave. When Sean was in middle school, his behavior worsened. He became skilled in conning his teachers and parents. The boy had no concern for the harm that his continuous deceptions and lies caused. These actions resulted in frustration, anger, and the undeserved guilt of his parents.

When Sean was confronted about his misbehavior, he usually blamed his teachers, friends, or family members for his predicament. He rarely took the blame for anything nor did he express guilt or remorse for his wrongdoings.

Sean had an eighteen-year-old brother and a fourteen-year-old sister, who both did well in school and had friends. Neither of them got into any unusual trouble at home or at school. Although there were no serious relationship problems between Sean and his siblings, they were not close.

Sean's experience in individual and family therapy could be described as uneventful. Although his school counselor believed that he had established a therapeutic relationship with Sean, he was unable to change any of his misbehaviors. Sean's activity in drug rehabilitation was also uneventful. Yet, he was considered to be a model client who caused no problems. Afterwards, however, he did not follow through with a drug or alcohol support group as recommended.

Sean's behavior during therapy and rehabilitation showed a young man who "played the system." He knew what was expected and he complied. His skill in conning and his ability in detecting what others wanted were superior. To get what he wanted, he would play the game. What he wanted was to resume his previous pattern of doing what he wanted to do exactly when he wanted to do it.

I began my approach to Sean's treatment by restructuring his parents' behavior patterns. I discussed Sean's dominant personality structure (Chapter 5) and the concept of anxiety (Chapter 3). With this information, they more effectively could combat Sean's uncaring antisocial behavior. They needed to know that Sean would have no incentive to make any of their desired changes as long as he felt no anxiety. It was also important for them to know that Sean's behavior might not change. They needed to understand that, even if he did make some notable changes, he might never become a loving, caring person.

The initial session dealt with educating the parents about the reality of just who Sean was and who he might become. Although this session was difficult for his parents, they felt a sense of relief in knowing that they had done everything that they could do in their attempts to help him throughout the years. It was also a relief for them to know that IT WAS NOT THEIR FAULT!

During the next session, Sean was confronted with the Improvement Program for Bad Children (Chapter 8). We outlined the maladaptive behavior that we targeted for change and discussed the consequences if he did not respond adequately. His response was, "That's stupid." During that week, his parents informed me that Sean had no difficulty at home or at school. I explained the concept of the "honeymoon period." This is the period of the calm before the storm. It was during the second week that the honeymoon ended. Sean was caught lying about homework and was strongly suspected of drug use. His parents quickly enacted the consequences of step four of the Improvement Program for Bad Children. They took away his three favorite privileges. Sean immediately attempted to con them with denial, lies, and promises. When they refused to listen, he had a temper outburst in an attempt to gain control. When he refused to discontinue his tirade, his parents responded by taking away all of his privileges for one week. That same night, Sean left home without any notice. When he did not return, I instructed the parents to contact the police and file a missing person's report. Two days later, Sean came home. He was in a good mood and acted as if nothing had happened. I advised the parents to offer him two choices: Enter another drug rehabilitation facility with follow-up treatments or find another place to live. Sean reacted with disbelief and then minimized the episode. His parents held firm in the choices that they had offered.

The importance of a highly organized and tightly knit structure cannot be underscored enough. Regaining control and offering limited choices is paramount in dealing with these troublesome children. Sean's choice at this phase could have gone either way. If Sean chose to live elsewhere, he would be provided with adult supervision. A family member could have assumed the task or the court could have provided supervision. If he chose drug rehab, he would be closely supervised after his stay was completed. The guidelines presented in the Improvement Program for Bad Children (detailed in Chapter 8) would be fully implemented. If he failed to comply and continued to be incorrigible, the choice to petition the court would be the alternative.

Sean chose to enter drug rehab. The staff at the rehabilitation facility was more confrontational than his teachers, school counselors, and parents. The staff knew about his earlier attempts to maintain a facade of compliance. Because Sean was in a tightly structured program, his parents were able to maintain better control of his attempts to manipulate and lie. In family therapy, they clearly stated what they expected when he returned to their home. They expected him to comply fully with his follow-up treatment and to obey the rules at home and school. Failure at this level would result in an application to the court for its supervision and Sean's placement in a residential setting.

For the first time, Sean took his parents seriously. He knew that they would do what they said. He no longer viewed them as merely threatening with no follow-through. Although he attempted to deceive them and resist their newly formed pattern of parenting, he did comply. His parents were satisfied with his response even though they never felt that he was a warm, caring, or loving son. His antisocial behaviors at school were extinguished along with his drug and alcohol use, but he still manipulated his classmates into following his suggestions. He also continued to display many of his previous dominant characteristics. Although much of the uncaring behavior was diminished, it was not extinguished.

Sean is a good example of the operator as outlined in Chapter 2. His expertise in wheeling, dealing, and manipulating; his dominant character; and his continual deceptions without concern for others made up a large component of his uncaring personality structure. What complicated issues more was his drug and alcohol abuse. It would have been impossible to work on his uncaring behaviors without first controlling the addiction.

In many instances, Sean's story could have turned out much differently. He could have resisted the family, school, and rehabilitation attempts to resolve the conflict. Had this been the case, Sean's parents would have had to go to court to press for state supervision of Sean. He would have been placed in a residential facility monitored by the state's department of children and youth services. Removal from his home would have meant that all of the other choices would have been denied to him. He would have been forced to comply with the standards, goals, and rules of that facility. His compliance or lack of compliance with the rules would have had a direct relationship to the privileges that he would receive. Only when his behavior was deemed as improved would he be considered able to regain his living status with his parents for a specified amount of time. For many hardcore, resistive, and uncaring children, the removal from their homes may be the best alternative.

According to former First Lady Nancy Reagan, "Drug and alcohol abuse touches all Americans in one form or another, but it is our children who are most vulnerable to its influence. (See "Bennett" on page P. iii.) As parents and teachers, we need to educate ourselves about the dangers of drugs so that we can teach our children. And we must go further still by convincing them that drugs are morally wrong."

I do not believe that it is enough to teach our children only the difference between right and wrong. It is admirable and noble to "Just Say No!" We live in an era when people spend millions of dollars for education about and prevention of drug and alcohol abuse. Since drug and alcohol use and abuse is multidimensional, we have enlisted the aid of schools, students, communities, and parents. Many instances have proved to be very successful.

Unfortunately, some dominant individuals lure children into drug abuse. As detailed in Chapter 5: Follow the Leader, the moderately dominant and subdominant individuals are more susceptible to and more easily influenced by dominant individuals. Furthermore, a 1983 Weekly Reader survey found that television and movies had the greatest influence in making drugs and alcohol seem attractive to fourth-graders; other children had the second greatest influence on them. When children were in the fifth and higher grades, their peers played an increasingly important role; television and movies consistently had the second greatest influence. The survey indicated that children who took drugs needed to "fit [in]," "feel older," and "have a good time." (See "Bennett" on page P. iii.)

Along with the usual preventative methods of helping our children to resist the temptation of drugs and alcohol use and abuse, the Schools Without Drugs work cited a number of schools that initiated a tough policy for students who were caught possessing or dealing drugs, Bennett (1986). Although a tough policy does not rid our society of this vile problem, it does give the right to an education to the majority of our children without their being jeopardized. The most effective school systems utilize the court system when dealing with users and dealers. Instead of school detention, the offenders are taken to court. Then, the parents are notified in order for them to assist in the rehabilitation of their children. The children's return to school is contingent upon the cooperation of the parents and the students' successful completion of the prescribed program.

If we are to attempt a successful intervention for an uncaring child, we must make certain that we can recognize and identify the early soft signs of misbehavior and the early signs of drug and alcohol use and abuse. Additionally, we must work closely with the school, community, and police for help with early prevention. If the uncaring child is allowed to escape our detection because of his drug and alcohol use, we then are faced with an even greater obstacle to combating his misconduct.

Chapter 7:
Attention Deficit Hyperactivity Disorder in Children and Adults

"Attention makes the genius; all learning, fancy, science, and skill depend upon it. Newton traced his great discoveries to it. It builds bridges, opens new worlds, heals diseases, carries on the business of the world. Without it taste is useless, and the beauties of literature unobserved."

Robert Willmott

Attention Deficit Hyperactivity Disorder (ADHD) is a diagnostic and descriptive category that refers to children of near average, average, or above average intellectual capacity with certain learning and/or behavioral disabilities ranging from mild to severe. These disabilities are associated with deviations of the functions of the central nervous system. The deviations may manifest themselves as various combinations of impairment in perception, conceptualization, language, memory, and control of attention, impulse, or motor function. This condition may arise from genetic variations, bio-chemical irregularities, perinatal brain insults, or other illnesses or injuries sustained during the years that are critical for the development and maturation of the central nervous system.

In the adult population, there is a growing concern about impairments in interpersonal relations, marriage, parenting, employment, and daily-life functioning. Many parents of children with ADHD and adults who suspect that they have the characteristics of ADHD are recognizing this disorder and seeking help.

Introduction

No concern should have a higher national priority than that of providing the fullest opportunities for physical and intellectual development for every child. Yet, for children suffering from Attention Deficit Disorder (ADD) or ADHD, the availability of special resources required for the accomplishment of this goal is extremely limited.

In every group of 100 school children, there are about five to ten who, despite average or above average intelligence, have a specific learning disability, hyperactivity, and/or other neuro-developmental irregularities that are severe enough to require special help. These children need all of the assistance that is possible for their disabilities and inefficiencies in learning. In addition, clinicians are becoming increasingly aware that ADHD in childhood does not dissipate in most afflicted individuals, but continues to hamper their adjustment into adulthood for over 50% of those cases. Therefore, it is imperative for mental health, medical, and educational professionals to have the most up-to-date knowledge of this disorder throughout their careers.

In the adult population, ADHD continues to impair interpersonal relations, marriages, careers, and interpersonal relationships. Many adults are recognizing this disorder and are seeking help. It is crucial that clinicians who specialize in adult disorders have the necessary skills and tools to deal with this newly emerging population of clients.

The physician has an important role in helping to identify and manage these children. Although the disabling symptoms and character traits of ADHD may be negligible when compared with the immediacy of serious prolonged physical illness, these disabilities are major obstacles for children who are trying to meet the demands of schools and modern society.

Thus, reaching the goals of identification, remediation, and treatment increases the child's chances for a productive and self-fulfilling adult life and prevents the development of emotional and psychological maladjustments.

Overview

During the 1950's and 1960's, children who were described as having "minimal brain dysfunction" (MBD) had certain limitations in their ability to modify their cognitive and motor functions (which are the reasoning and muscle functions), but their intelligence levels usually were well above the range designated as mentally retarded.

MBD was based on the concept that there are brain abnormalities that underlie and correspond to observed symptoms. This concept did not commit itself to a particular cause of brain dysfunction. This concept did not preclude the possibility of other psychological difficulties in the child. Nor did this concept propose that other brain irregularities or dysfunctions were not present. In fact, many children with cerebral palsy, epilepsy, or organic brain impairment had symptoms in common with MBD. The difference is that, in the more severe disabilities (such as cerebral palsy, brain damage, and epilepsy), the motor system (and often the cognitive system) is impaired in a gross manner. In MBD, the deficits were less obvious and characteristically related to subtle integrations and differentiations of positioning, movement, and cognition.

The concept of MBD was developed because:

(1) Many children had the characteristic symptoms and behaviors without a definitive history of brain damage.

(2) At the time that the concept of MBD was being developed in the 1950's and 1960's, children who were referred to child guidance clinics were treated as if the hyperactivity and cognitive deficits were caused entirely by interpersonal transactions. Thus, the child and his parents were assigned to psychotherapy as the treatment of choice without consideration of other causes and treatments.

(3) Neither the schools nor the physicians had the concepts that were needed to assume responsibility for these children.

(4) Although quite a few specialists recognized hyperkinetic syndrome (a hyperactivity disability) and developmental dyslexia (a learning disability), a much larger number of children showed a mixture of both of these disabilities in a remarkable range from the very mild to the very severe. There was confusion about what to call these various types of children with problems of learning and hyperkinesias. Minimal brain dysfunction became the term that was used most widely.

The 1960's journal articles that discussed evaluation emphasized the necessity for a team of child specialists (frequently called a child study team or unit). This team commonly included a pediatric neurologist, a child psychiatrist, a clinical psychologist, an educational diagnostician, a language specialist, and a social worker. Such evaluation teams usually existed only in large medical complexes and even those could not possibly evaluate the large number of children that were referred.

In the 1970's, two major changes occurred that helped to simplify the situation. First: An educational category named "specific learning disabilities" was developed. Due to this classification, the requirement for a medical diagnosis to provide services within the schools was no longer needed. Second: The assessment process was carefully reviewed again. The result was the elimination of the procedures that didn't contribute significantly either to diagnosis or to treatment planning.

Attention Deficit Hyperactivity Disorder

Diagnosis of ADHD is based on three areas:

A. impulsiveness – does not learn from consequences of actions

B. inattentiveness or distractibility

C. hyperactivity

The following is the ADHD criteria as outlined in the Diagnostic and Statistical Manual of Mental Disorders published by the American Psychiatric Association in 1994:

1. Six or more of the following symptoms of inattention have persisted for at least six months to a degree that is maladaptive and inconsistent with developmental level:

Inattention

    a. often fails to give close attention to details or makes careless mistakes in schoolwork, work, or other activity.

    b. often has difficulty sustaining attention tasks or play activties

    c. often does not seem to listen when spoken to directly

    d. often does not follow through on instructions and fails to finish schoolwork, chores, or duties in the workplace (not due to oppositional behavior or failure to understand instructions)

    e. often has difficulty organizing tasks and activities

    f. often avoids, dislikes, or is reluctant to engage in tasks that require sustained mental effort (such as schoolwork or or homework)

    g. often loses things that are necessary for tasks or activities (such as toys, school assignments, pencils, books, and tools)

    h. often easily distracted by extraneous stimuli

    i. often forgetful in daily activities

2. Six or more of the following symptoms of hyperactivity-impulsivity

have persisted for at least six months to a degree that is malada
tive and inconsistent with developmental level:

Hyperactivity

    a. often fidgets with hands or feet or squirms in seat

    b. often gets out of seat in classroom or in other locations where
remaining seated is expected

    c. often runs about or climbs excessively in situations where it
is inappropriate (may be limited to subjective feelings of
restlessness

    d. often has difficulty playing or engaging in leisure activities
quietly

    e. often "on the go" or often acts as if "driven by a motor"

    f. often talks excessively

Impulsivity

    g. often blurts out answers before questions
have been completed

    h. often has difficulty awaiting turn

    i. often interrupts or intrudes on others (such as butting into
conversations or games)

B. Some hyperactive-impulsive symptoms or inattentive
symptoms that caused impairment were present before
age of seven years.

C. Some impairment from the symptoms is present in two or
more settings (such as at school, daycare, or home).

D. There must be clear evidence of clinically significant
impairment in social, academic, or home functioning.

E. The symptoms do not occur exclusively during the course of a
pervasive developmental disorder, schizophrenia, or other
psychotic disorder and are not better accounted for by another
mental disorder (such as a mood or personality disorder).

Interviewing of Parents

The review of pre-assessment data from the school and family
prior to the office visit can be most helpful in evaluating past events

and present contributing factors that relate to the child's referral. The information on the forms allows the clinician to concentrate on pertinent areas, personalizes the assessment procedure, and becomes a permanent record.

There is no substitute for the in-depth initial interview with parents because it obtains the history of the child and the symptoms or behavioral characteristics. However, forms previously completed by the family and the school shorten the procedure by focusing on problem areas.

ADHD cannot be diagnosed accurately on the basis of a brief office examination and a hurried description of current behavior and achievement. ADHD doesn't happen suddenly at any particular age. A person is born with ADHD. It is not an acquired behavior. It may present itself due to a variety of causes, such as prolonged physical illness or severe emotional trauma.

Obviously, ADHD children also are subject to physical illnesses and environmental traumas. Perhaps, they are even more sensitive to it. Their maladjustments are physiological and may have their origins in heredity, birth trauma, or events in early childhood. It is this type of historical information that can contribute greatly to the diagnosis.

Diagnostic Screening

The search for a psychological assessment package specific to children with learning and behavior deviations due to ADHD generally has been unproductive. This circumstance is the result of the varying nature of the disability and the variety of symptoms or traits that diversely manifest in a variety of children and at different ages. The selection of appropriate tests is determined by taking into account such factors as the age of the child, chief complaints, major symptoms or traits, data from other sources, school placement possibilities, and other services that are available.

Certain procedures are basic to psychological evaluation. Among these are individual appraisals of general intelligence; current inventories of the basic academic skill; measures of complex perceptual functioning; behavioral descriptions; and additional indices of language, learning, and behavior.

Psychological evaluation is necessary to assure parents, physicians, learning disabilities teachers, and program directors that the child's general intellectual level is near or within the average range and that the potential for higher achievement is present. Additionally, the clinical assessment can help to isolate the areas of impaired function that may be corrected by specific training methods.

Because it is difficult to assess ADHD by using the most common diagnostic screening tools, I developed a diagnostic screening test that is designed to determine whether or not ADHD exists. In 2001, I determined that, with the development and utilization of Diagnostic Screening Inventory for Children & Adults (DSICA) and with the accompanying tests (below), there is a greater predictability of providing an accurate diagnosis along with specific and appropriate treatment planning. The DSICA differentiates between clinical symptoms and maladaptive behaviors. Much of the clinical confusion lies in enmeshing the two meanings. The DSICA clears up this misunderstanding by showing the difference between the symptoms from the behaviors. As a result, proper treatment can be prescribed for each individual. The importance of realizing that the symptoms must be separated from the behaviors cannot be overemphasized. When treating symptoms, especially those of severe depression where there may be a risk of death, there is no logical reason for attempting to remove undesirable behaviors if the patient has a high probability of committing suicide. This most important aspect must be addressed first. The DSICA then collates the clinical information for immediate dissemination to the parents for their review and for appropriate treatment planning.

With the utilization of diagnostic screening tests, I now am able to determine where children more accurately can be placed with regard to accurate diagnoses, specific areas of impairment, and credible treatment plans.

IMPORTANT STATISTICAL INFORMATION

- An estimated three to seven percent of school-aged children and four percent of the adults in the United States – more than eight million people – have ADHD.

- Males are two to three times more likely to be diagnosed than girls. Girls may be under-diagnosed.

- The child's behavior in the doctor's office may be different from that at home or school.

- Children with ADHD might be able to focus on television or video games for one to two hours.

- Children with ADHD might have associated learning disorders. Psycho-educational testing should be considered if this is suspected.

- Treatment of co-morbid disorders is necessary, such as for dyslexia, behavioral problems, and depression.

- 50% of children with ADHD continue to have problems when they become adults.

- Adults suspected of having ADHD should have psychiatric and psychological treatment.

Diagnosis of ADHD Is Based on Three Areas:

1. Impulsiveness – does not learn from consequences of actions
2. Inattentiveness or Distractibility
3. Hyperactivity – does not need to be hyperactive to have ADHD

Observations leading to a referral for and identification of ADHD frequently are not made until the child has attended school for the first few years, even though there may have been previous suspicious behaviors that went unattended.

There are two areas in which abnormalities may be precursors of learning and/or behavioral problems in school. The first and most easily identifiable is a deviation in the levels of activity of the children. The abnormalities are in the quantity and quality of motor (muscle) activities. The most frequently observed dysfunction is excessive non-goal-related motor activity. Less commonly observed ones are cases of abnormally low levels of activities with poor focus toward goals. Many parents assume that because their children are able to concentrate on specific play activities for long periods, they cannot have ADHD. This conclusion may be far from the truth regarding this condition. This simple example will illustrate how children might perceive their situations: Compare children's motor activity to that of a speeding engine going 100 miles an hour. If the activity that they choose is going about the same speed, there should be no perceived conflict between the children and the activity. However, if the activity is going significantly slower than the children's speed, the children will become seriously conflicted, disturbed, and bored with the activity. They soon will lose interest and will become distracted by an abundance of sounds, activities, or perceived annoyances from his parents.

The second area of abnormality is delayed language development. It appears safe to speculate that children who fail to achieve normal development in the use of language will have learning disabilities in school. Delayed or atypical language development is the most reliable predictor of specific learning disabilities in the future. Thus, the clinician should be alert to the early signs of these developmental delays.

Management of ADHD

Clinicians' roles in management vary from the simple to the complex depending upon their personal inclinations, the nature and extent of the children's problems, and accessible community resources.

Their responsibilities include the interpretation of the diagnoses to families and others; medication management; collaboration with schools, families, and others; and referrals of families to other professionals for specialized therapies.

Modalities of Treatment

The treatment forms that are presently available for comprehensive management of ADHD are classified into four broad groupings:

I. Educational
    A. Regular (modified)
    B. Special education programs for Specific Learning
       Disabilities (SLD)
       1. Resource room
       2. Self-contained classroom
       3. Itinerant teacher/consultant
    C. Private tutoring

II. Specific Training Programs for Central Processing Function

III. Medical
    A. Collaborative case management

B. Special medication

IV. Psychiatric, Psychological, and Social Therapies
    A. Individual child psychotherapy
    B. Parent psychotherapy
    C. Family group therapy
    D. Child and family management counseling

Any or all of the above may be necessary for a particular ADHD child in a particular family constellation at some point in time. Unfortunately, it will be a rare situation in which these different treatments are available to the family within a delivery system. Priorities in treatment programming then can be established based upon the availability of treatments in the local community.

I. Educational

Regular

In this method of treatment within the school system, children remain in regular classrooms, but receive a slight modification of curriculum and management. These might include more personal attention, a slower pace of teaching, fewer explicit requirements, the repeat of one grade during the elementary years, or twelve-month education for one or more years. Schools may provide additional services, such as speech therapy or remedial reading. Although regular educational treatment may be enough for children with minor deviations in learning and behavior, it is rarely sufficient for those with more pronounced symptoms. These children will require more intensified and structured approaches.

Special

ADHD children with moderate deviations in learning and behavior frequently are programmed for what has become known as "resource rooms," a unique approach that was developed first at the elementary school level.

The resource room requires the skills of a teacher who knows the symptoms that are in the category of ADHD and who is specifically trained to teach and manage such children. The children remain in their regular grades, but go to their resource room teachers on a daily basis at specific times. The periods vary from thirty minutes to two hours during which individualized training and instruction are provided. The training and instruction are based on the children's functioning levels and primary areas of deficit. This may be done with a single child or with small groups of children with similar needs. Such placement requires close cooperation between the regular classroom teacher and the resource room teacher.

A second form of special education treatment is the self-contained classroom for those children with severe symptoms of ADHD. These children remain with a specially trained teacher for the entire school day.

The special education model must provide for upward movement from one program to another when the child has made sufficient progress.

Within these basic educational treatment models, various special strategies have been utilized, such as the use of teaching aides or volunteers for particular services to individual children, cross-age teaching, and the buddy system. In the buddy system, an ADHD child is paired with a peer whose deportment and academic ability are considered above average and who serves as a helpmate and model. Other strategies include team-teaching, open classroom, taped textbooks (or compassionate readers for a reading-disordered child so that content can be acquired), and behavior modification techniques.

In some school districts, a teacher with special training in specific learning disabilities is employed to serve several schools as a consultant to regular teachers. This teacher travels from school to school and helps to develop an individualized program for particular SLD children that can be implemented by the regular classroom teacher. This teacher may suggest specific materials, methods of teaching specific skills, program changes, management techniques, and other procedures.

Usually, this specialized teacher does not work directly with the children, but serves as a consultant to other school personnel, an agent for change, and an advocate for SLD children.

Private Tutoring

In those instances when no public school services for ADHD children are available or when additional educational treatment is necessary, private tutoring may be arranged. Parents usually contract this service privately. Parents should be encouraged to work with school personnel when securing a qualified tutor. Very often, retired teachers, particularly those who taught the early elementary grades, are utilized in this fashion.

II. Specific Training for Central Processing Functions

As the field of ADHD developed and became more refined, it was natural that there would be an increase in the development of assessment techniques that claim to measure those deficits in specific central processing functions within the central nervous system (CNS). It followed that the next step would be a proliferation of specific training activities, methods, and materials designed to offer a seemingly direct attack on these specific areas of deficit, particularly visual perception, as well as auditory perception, cross-modality integrations, and motor coordination and skills.

These treatment forms are widely used throughout the country. They often are blended into the various daily activities of children in resource rooms or self-contained classrooms within public schools. If such training is not emphasized to the satisfaction of the parents or if the child is not making the amount of progress for which the parents are hoping, these services frequently are contracted on a private basis.

Concern about an ADHD child makes parents exceedingly vulnerable to a host of questionable and expensive cult-oriented treatment approaches. The effectiveness of these training methods in altering CNS functioning or in facilitating the acquisition of basic academic skills is yet to be established firmly. However, they do provide a framework for structuring activities and remedial instruction that are different from those in which the child has failed. Because these more directly relate to the child's specific disabilities, they can make a contribution to treatment.

III. Medical

A. Collaborative Case Management

In some ADHD cases, school and family collaboration along with special medication is the preferred treatment plan. Particularly in the beginning of this treatment approach, close attention to particulars of the case and frequent interchange of information among physician, school, and family are required until it is established that the medication is maximally effective. Poor communication should not be allowed to delay or obscure the anticipated results.

B. Special Medication

Medication is not indicated for every ADHD child. Consideration should be given to a trial of medication when other remedial measures alone are insufficient and the following criteria for ADHD have been met: (1) intelligence level is near average, average, or above average; (2) school performance and/or behavior is significantly below that which is expected for child's age and measured intelligence; (3) some combination of the typical traits of ADHD are present (short attention span, hyperactivity, perceptual-motor impairments, general coordination deficits, impulsivity, "soft" neurological signs); and (4) absence of serious emotional disturbance.

IV. Psychiatric, Psychological, and Social Therapies

Because of certain circumstances surrounding particular families containing one or more ADHD children, it is not unusual that, during certain periods of stress, individual psychotherapy or counseling with the child and/or parents may be required. Sometimes, family group therapy is needed.

Also included in this form of intervention would be special consultation with schools and teachers by knowledgeable physicians, social workers, psychologists, education specialists, language specialists, behavior-shaping technologists, and other professionals.

Psychotropic Medications

There has been a great controversy about the use of certain food additives, diets, and medications in treating hyperactive children. Although there are treatment methods that can help hyperactive children, many youngsters are prevented from having proper treatment due to myths, fears, and misinformation.

Dr. Charles Bradley, one of the pioneers in the use of stimulant medication for behavior-disordered children, reported in 1937, "A large proportion of the children became emotionally subdued without, however, losing interest in their surroundings... Possibly the most spectacular change in behavior...was the remarkable improvement in school performance of approximately half of the children."

By the 1950's, the development of Dexedrine (dextroamphetamine) and Ritalin (methoylphenidate) came into common use for the treatment of ADHD. There are many who believe that stimulants given to children merely tranquilize them. Stimulants do not tranquilize or sedate hyperactive children. They assist the children in focusing their attention. They help to organize and regulate their levels of activity and behavior. It is estimated that 80% or more of hyperactive children show improvement across a broad range of behavior.

For decades, medications have been used to treat the "symptoms" of ADHD. I don't prefer the term "symptoms" when referring to the concept of treatment for ADHD children. Instead, when discussing the criteria for such children, I choose to use "maladaptive character traits or behaviors." I view symptoms as complaints by the patients and maladaptive behaviors as complaints by the parents and society.

The medications that appear to be prescribed the most are a class of drugs known as stimulants. They are as follows:

Brand Name	Generic Name	Aproved Age in Years
Adderall	Amphetamine	3 and older
Concerta	Methylphenidate	6 and older
Cylert	Pemoline	6 and older
Dexedrine	Dextroamphetamine	3 and older
Dextrostat	Dextroamphetamine	3 and older
Focalin	Dexmethylphenidate	6 and older
Metadate ER	Methylphenidate ER	6 and older
Metadate CD	Methylphenidate ER	6 and older

Brand Name	Generic Name	Aproved Age in Years
Ritalin	Methylphenidate	6 and older
Ritalin SR	Methylphenidate ER	6 and older
Ritalin LA	Methylphenidate LA	6 and older

Of special importance is the fact that stimulant medication does not cease to be helpful during adolescence. About 50% to 60% of adults who are hyperactive or diagnosed with ADHD benefit from stimulant treatment.

Side Effects:
1. poor appetite
2. insomnia
3. headaches
4. stomachache

On October 23, 2003, research scientists discovered that a new ADHD medication, Strattera, caused fewer sleep disturbances and worked better for children who also have a tic disorder – a sudden, rapid, recurrent, and non-rhythmic motor movement or vocalization. Strattera was the first non-stimulant medication approved by the US Food and Drug Administration (FDA) for the treatment of ADHD in children, adolescents, and adults. Strattera is a norepinephrine reuptake inhibitor, a class of ADHD treatment that works differently from the other available ADHD medications.

Mary Ann

Mary Ann was a hyperactive, stubborn, demanding, and ill tempered six year old. During her first year of life, she refused to be held, cuddled, or loved. She cried at her mother's attempts to breastfeed her. She was equally impossible to bottle-feed and resorted to spitting out almost all of her formula.

Mary Ann's mother was an intravenous drug user and was addicted to alcohol before, during, and after the pregnancy. Mary Ann was born prematurely due to her mother's bleeding during pregnancy. She was also a fussy baby who screamed most of the time.

After the first year, Mary Ann's mother lost custody to the child's grandparents. During the following years, she became increasingly more stubborn, demanding, and mischievous. She would not listen to her grandparents and made their lives miserable.

When I first saw MaryAnn, I found her to be quite exasperating. She got into everything in my office without regard for its value or her own harm. She explored electric chords and sockets. She jumped on the furniture. Any attempts to caution or stop her resulted in further exploration, opposition, or contempt. Her grandparents told me about her demand to sleep in their room rather than her own. She refused to go to bed at the required time. Moreover, she would not eat most of the food that they prepared or share any of her playthings with her peers. Their attempts to control her misbehavior became a discouraging full-time job.

Mary Ann's teacher was concerned about her playing by herself. When other children attempted to play with her, she would become demanding, selfish, and mean. Her teacher also noted her hyperactivity and poor attention span. She had great difficulty in staying in one place while performing one activity. She was always in a state of motion. Any noise or movement of the other children easily distracted her. She grabbed the playthings of her peers without considering their ownership. She had quick emotional swings from happy to angry to whiny. There were also some noticeable difficulties in her fine motor coordination. She was unable to color within the lines as well as the average child of her age could. Of noteworthy importance was that many who knew her said that she would show remorse and guilt whenever she was scolded. Her teachers and grandparents strongly believed that she was a caring and loving child, but her hyperactive and impulsive behavior prevented these emotions.

Mary Ann represents many children whose addicted mothers create great difficulties for their offspring. The mother's habitual use and abuse of drugs and alcohol were the primary causes of her daughter's problem behaviors. Her condition was referred to as Attention Deficit Hyperactivity Disorder. In most instances, it is quite difficult to determine the cause of this condition largely due to the lack of medical evidence in spite of medical and psychological testing.

To determine the presence of ADHD, data from the school and family can be most helpful. ADHD cannot be evaluated on the basis of a brief office examination. ADHD does not occur suddenly at a certain age. Antisocial behavior and/or poor school performance may not be related to ADHD. It may have been caused by other factors, such as an emotional disorder or a physical illness. The ADHD child's major problem is a physiological one that is caused by heredity, pregnancy influences, birth trauma, or a circumstance or circumstances in early childhood. In Mary Ann's situation, we have evidence of a mother's drug and alcohol abuse prior to and during pregnancy. There are problem behaviors at birth (including crying at her mother's attempts to breastfeed; spitting out her formula; and refusing to be held, cuddled, or loved) and current behaviors that describe ADHD. Although Mary Ann's behaviors certainly are similar to descriptions of the uncaring child, her expressions of guilt and remorse make it highly unlikely that she is in that group of children. This distinction separates her from the Uncaring Child Syndrome and places her into the category of ADHD.

CONCLUSION

Mental health clinicians see a vast number of individuals who have the characteristics of ADHD. As the general public becomes more knowledgeable about the traits associated with ADHD, all clinicians need to become more clinically prepared to meet this ever-growing challenge. Each professional needs to be skilled in the diagnostic screening tools that are available and know how to make sound and helpful interpretations of the test results. Additionally, each must be able to provide adequate treatment planning and case management to the children with ADHD and to those adults with similar clinical characteristics.

Both the public and clinicians are becoming increasingly aware that ADHD in childhood does not disappear, but continues to manifest itself throughout adulthood. Without proper intervention, ADHD may result in broken marriages, lost jobs, interpersonal difficulties, and a host of other significant problems. Mental health clinicians have the responsibility of learning as much up-to-date knowledge about this disorder as possible.

Chapter 8:
The Treatment Process:
Dr. Hoffman's Improvement Program for Bad Children

"What's done to children they will do to society."
Karl Menninger

Freudian psychoanalytic theory proposes that the most important events in determining personality structure and psychiatric illness occur during the first seven years of the person's life. Dr. Sigmund Freud believed that each child could be impacted by environment and biological constitution. He was the first to suggest that a special relationship exists between the biology of the individual and that person's environment. In other words, he felt that a child's psychiatric illness could be caused by both childhood experiences and the child's own biological makeup.

In the Freudian tradition, patients are expected to see their analysts four or five times a week for several years. They lie on couches, are encouraged to say whatever they want to their therapists, who remain neutral in order not to influence their patients' spontaneous verbal productions. Consequently, the spontaneous verbal productions, called "free association," produce patterns of hidden thoughts, conflicts, and insights, which eventually lead to a "cure."

In 1951, the late Carl Rogers, the "client centered" therapist, focused on face to face therapy rather than having the patient lie on the couch. He called people "clients," not patients, so that they were not demeaned as ill. Rogerian therapists are much more active with their clients than Freudian psychoanalysts. Techniques involve restating and summarizing what the client says in an attempt to promote insight and growth while keeping them more focused on their treatment.

During the 1950's and 1960's, a number of therapists set out to raise the consciousness of society, Perls, Hefferline and Goodman (1951).

The "Human Growth Movement," as it was called, was expected to give new experiences to the participants by allowing them to feel, touch, and freely express their hidden thoughts, anger, ideas, and fantasies.

Behavior modification came of age during the late 1960's and early 1970's. In 1953, B.F. Skinner, an American psychologist, first brought the concept of Operant Conditioning into modern focus. He developed conditioning techniques that used rewards or the withdrawal of punishment when the subject performed a desired behavior. His experiments progressed from laboratory experiments with animals to human beings. Applications of these techniques in treatment and education flourished through the years, Staats and Staats (1963).

Behavioral Management (Modification)

I have designed the following behavioral modification program – the Improvement Program for Bad Children – with options so that it can be utilized for uncaring children. A case study will be presented later as one example.

For decades, childrearing methods have remained virtually the same. These methods constantly place heavy emphases on the parents to win the cooperation of the children and to be good listeners. Specific elements (such as empathy, genuine regard, respect, and warmth) are called reflective responses and are the cornerstones of self help parenting books and instructional courses. Unfortunately, these materials fail to deal effectively with the "Uncaring Child Syndrome," although they often prove helpful for children whose behaviors are not as serious.

A detailed, six step treatment process is outlined and discussed in this chapter. A comprehensive examination of children's current behaviors, attitudes, and feelings is delineated clearly. I also provide information about possible roles that parents might adopt in relation to children. In this way, parents can identify characteristics and respond to children's exhibited behaviors. I offer a step by step process to correct children's maladaptive behaviors and to strengthen parents' marital relationships and/or support networks.

The volume of material dealing with parenting issues has impressed me throughout my 43 years of clinical experience. I have attended many varieties of workshops, parent effectiveness courses, and lectures on the subject that were inadequate. Unfortunately, the information offered through such sources is not consistent and is ineffective in dealing with the uncaring child.

This chapter is intended as a resource for parents, relatives, educators, clinicians, and all who are involved with children. This chapter explains the role of support groups and provides guidelines for selecting an appropriate therapist. Too often, parents spend unnecessary time and money enlisting the aid of therapists who are ill equipped to assist them in coping with such children. Instead of helping the family, some therapists may exacerbate an already-deteriorating situation. I believe that the resource information in this chapter will provide help and hope for anyone involved with an uncaring child.

Step One: Target Behaviors

Make a list of the target problem behaviors. That is, list the behaviors that you believe to be disruptive and unhealthy. Arrange them according to their level of importance. For example:

1. lies
2. earns failing grades
3. ignores or "forgets" chores
4. exhibits inappropriate anger
5. is argumentative
6. curses
7. is inattentive
8. has temper outbursts
9. excessively uses phone
10. does not follow the rules
11. has bad manners
12. is irresponsible
13. is rude and insulting
14. bullies and mistreats younger brother or sister
15. mistreats pets
16. teases
17. steals or takes things
18. cheats
19. is disobedient and uncooperative
20. uses drugs and/or alcohol

21. does not come home at the required times
22. runs away
23. is physically and/or verbally abusive

Your list will highlight the problem behaviors that are disturbing to the household and will help to develop a therapeutic approach that is simple and free of obstacles.

The following case study will illustrate how the Improvement Program for Bad Children can dramatically improve behavior.

Mike

When Mike came to my office, he displayed behaviors like those in the Step One list. A fourteen year old middle child in a family of three children, he was the only one who displayed disruptive behavior in the household and at school. His parents told me that he lied about having any homework to do in spite of failing grades. He became argumentative, angry, and used profanity whenever his parents approached him about his grades and homework. He made excuses for not doing his chores. His teachers reported that he did not pay attention to instructions and usually was socializing too much with his peers. He rarely helped with the family chores and spent an excessive amount of time playing, watching television, playing video games, and talking on the phone with his friends.

Mike's uncooperativeness had been going on since he was two years old. His parents had little success in gaining his cooperation. Most of their prior attempts at making things better involved talking and appealing to his sense of understanding and fairness to everyone. When this failed, they tried to punish him by grounding him. When frustrated by his lack of positive change, they responded by yelling and threatening.

The foregoing scenario is quite common in the American family. The list that was detailed earlier helps to identify the target behaviors that need to be extinguished. Parents can use it to determine what should be changed. This list must be modified in accordance to the parents' priorities and needs and to the child's particular behaviors.

Step Two: Privileges and Pleasures

Make a list of the child's pleasures and privileges – ideally with the child's input – and arrange them in any order. For example:

1. playing with friends
2. video games
3. television
4. music
5. clothes
6. karate lessons
7. use of automobile
8. allowance
9. special food
10. gifts
11. hobbies
12. use of telephone
13. special trips/vacations
14. movies

After making your list of privileges and pleasures, arrange them (with the assistance of your child, if possible) in the order of priority ranging from the activity or possession that they value the most to the one least treasured.

Step Three: Warning!!!

Tell your children that, if they persist in any of the top three behaviors listed in Step One: Target Behaviors, you will restrict them from the list of Step Two: Privileges and Pleasures for a specific length of time. It is of utmost importance that you do not discuss this issue at length. Your child may attempt to talk to you in order to divert your attention or may try to make you feel guilty. If either happens, warn your child only one time. If your child fails to comply, make your move. Do it with firm conviction in a matter-of-fact manner. Do not yell or make repeated threats. The warning should be in a calm but deliberate tone of voice that denotes confidence. Do not attempt to use it as a fear tactic or to instill guilt. Also, avoid expressing anger and punitive statements. The manner in which you approach your children should be casual and non threatening.

Step Four: Consequences

When you learn of any violations of Step One: Target Behaviors, swiftly restrict the top three of Step Two: Privileges and Pleasures in a calm but firm manner. The length of time that your children's privileges are removed depends on the severity of the violations. The length generally runs from three to six hours or from one day to one week. The time should be longer for more serious conditions. If your children's behaviors persist during the time of their restrictions or if additional conflicts arise from your attempts to rectify their misbehaviors, all of the privileges of Step Two: Privileges and Pleasures should be restricted. During the time of the penalties, do not engage in any discussions about the violations, the restriction of privileges, and any other related issues. These discussions must take place only at the conclusion of the penalties. Discussions with children during the penalty phase will contaminate the effect of the consequences. In fact, if the children persist in discussing their dilemmas, tell them that you will not discuss anything until the termination of their penalties. Emphasize that the penalties will become longer and the remaining privileges will be terminated if they mention it again. Remember that your children are the masters of deception. If there were a college degree for this type of behavior, each most certainly would receive a Ph.D.

Step Five: Overcorrection

Frequently, taking away privileges and pleasures is ineffective in getting your message noticed. Occasionally, we have to take more drastic steps to gain children's attention and cause enough discomfort within them to make the necessary change. Overcorrection is the use of multiple consequences when a lack of compliance occurs. For example, if your children fail to comply in spite of taking away all of their privileges and pleasures, overcorrection is enforced in the following manner: Add a long list of chores that your children must complete before they regain their privileges and pleasures. You might say to your child, "While you are grounded for the next 24 hours, you will not have the privilege of watching television, listening to your music, using the telephone, leaving the house, or receiving visits from your friends AND you also will be expected to perform five chores on this list before your privileges are reinstated." Create your own list and include as many chores as you want. You can decide how many chores must be performed based on the level of your child's offense. Below are some examples.

1. clean your room
2. clean the bathrooms (including toilet bowls)
3. wash the car
4. wash the dishes
5. vacuum the carpet
6. dust the living room, the family room, and bedrooms
7. wax the floor in the dining room

Step Six: Reward

When you believe that your children are responding positively to the consequences of their behaviors – when there are positive changes – it is essential for you to reward them with hugs, pats on their backs, and a few positive remarks. Do not overdo your praise! You then can reinstate all of their privileges from Step Two: Privileges and Pleasures.

When Mike was presented with the discussion as outlined in Step Three: Warning, he said, "This is stupid." After his attempts to stop his parent's intervention failed, Mike settled down and complied. About ten days later, one of Mike's teachers informed his parents that he was not doing his homework and was failing. When his parents approached him, he became angry, cursed, and stomped out of the house. When he returned, his parents repeated Step Three: Warning. During that week, Mike's parents caught him in several lies and determined that he was not doing homework and "forgetting" to do his chores. He sulked and was belligerent. Mike was told that all of his privileges were being restricted until his three primary problems in Step One: Target Behaviors were resolved.

As parents, you have the vitally important responsibility of determining how many target problem behaviors should be considered for elimination. When you are faced with continued resistance and defiance of fair expectations, eliminate one pleasure or privilege at a time until you have the child's full compliance.

The weeks that followed were difficult. Mike's parents faced guilt for restricting their son's "normal" existence. At times, they talked about reinstating some of his privileges in spite of his non compliance. I supported them through telephone consultations at least four times each week.

Several weeks later, Mike made his drastic change. He began coming home with his textbooks and discontinued swearing and lying. His teachers indicated an improvement in his grades and attitude. Mike's parents enacted Step Six: Reward and reinstated all of his privileges.

Mike slipped several times throughout the year. He periodically needed the reminders in Step Four: Consequences to bring him back into compliance. Joyfully, his parents remarked, "We now have a son and a future."

In observing the success in Mike's treatment process, we must not look towards his experiencing guilt or remorse for his misbehaviors. If we are to be successful, we must produce controlled discomfort. Even this mild to moderate degree of anxiety is never wished for or wanted. Mike certainly did not look forward to losing his privileges. When he discovered that his parents could not be intimidated nor manipulated, he had only two choices. One, continue to be without or, two, comply and make certain concessions that would restore his lost privileges. Mike chose to keep his privileges and comply with his parents' expectations. They were fortunate. Many parents discover that their uncaring children refuse to buy into their parent's needs and expectations regardless of how fair they may be. Mike graduated from high school and attended community college. Although Mike and his parents continued to have difficulties in their relationship, his parents felt a sense of relief that he had activated positive behaviors by setting healthy and meaningful future goals.

The Improvement Program for Bad Children is designed to help parents respond effectively to tumultuous and disruptive behavior. This system successfully simplifies parent/child conflicts.

SPECIAL CONSIDERATION

Remarriage

During the 1980's and into the 1990's, there was an increase in the number of remarried families. Remarriage can create problems in the roles of family members. Who is who in this newly blended family? Children often resent "the intruder," the non biological parent, whom they designate as the villain. They often feel displaced in their traditional positions and feel threatened when change is suggested. At the same time, natural parents feel a special alliance to their own children and easily may be manipulated by a child who wants to be rescued from the stepparent. If this occurs, the marriage partners soon begin to battle. The wedge between them then widens as greater turmoil erupts within the entire family, which allows the child to escape responsibility while pitting one parent against the other.

In spite of earlier psychological teachings insisting that parents speak as "one voice" and maintain mutual agreement when raising their children, my experience with remarried families having to deal with uncaring children does not fit this traditional mold. My advice to the remarried parents of an uncaring child, as well as most children, is that they accept different roles when it comes to discipline. The biological parent should be the one who manages the discipline, thereby reducing the chance of contamination and helping to prevent the dividing of parental loyalties (called triangulation). The use of this method reduces difficulties before they can become major problems. Therefore, parental bickering about issues unrelated to the child's behavior must be avoided. The non biological parent must be removed as the one who is responsible for expanding the current crisis. The non biological parent might complicate an already difficult situation.

Natural Parents

Contrary to the advice that I give to remarried parents, I suggest strongly that natural parents work together and take a mutual position when it comes to the rearing of their children. Unlike with remarried parents, children who have both biological parents have a much clearer perception of the roles within the family. Unless we are dealing with dysfunctional parents, the roles of the children have not become jeopardized by the "intrusion" of a new surrogate parent. Their parents are the same people who have been with them from the beginning. Therefore, the natural parents must unite to demonstrate a mutual understanding and authority that can be used as a model by their children.

Single Parents

Prior to the mid-1940's, the majority of people knew what a mother and father were "supposed" to do. Children had their roles regarding participating in school and assisting with family chores. With the arrival of the 1950's came a freer time without a depression or a world war. The 1950's represented a happier time for the family in America. There was a greater feeling of family togetherness. The 1960's ushered in the Vietnam War, a wider usage of drugs, a huge increase in premarital and extramarital sex, and the beginning of the end of the traditional family. Families relocated for financial reasons and to live in more desirable surroundings. Significantly greater numbers of mothers began working and helping with the family finances. Many families began depending upon two salaries just to exist. As the roles became more uncertain, stress increased and the nation's economic status worsened. Divorce increased dramatically. As the divorce rate increased, its effect on American children became more noticeable. Not only did the parents experience the crisis, but the children did, too. Single parents experienced financial decline, emotional and physical stress, depression, anger, rage, agitation, and fear about their children's emotional harm.

Many parents ask me, "Will our children do better if we stay together until they are grown?" The majority of children from broken homes tell me that they wish that their parents had remained together. They feel that their lives were ruined due to divorce. Most children disapprove of any change in their environment. Of course, in various unhealthy situations, divorce is often better for children.

When the change of the magnitude of a divorce occurs, the family structure is traumatized much of the time. Failing grades, depression, and anger might result when children are subjected to the dissolution of their parent's marriage. Therefore, it is extremely important to empower these children with the customary roles that they previously performed. In other words, do not change the child's duties or responsibilities because of the change of mates.

When single parents are faced with disciplining an uncaring child, the task often is complicated by guilt. For instance, a single mother might attempt to offset any perceived emotional harm caused by the divorce. If she feels that her children are in danger of experiencing depression, she usually will try to rescue her children from this pain. Therefore, the single parent might retreat from forcing the children to face the consequences of their misbehaviors. If the single mother and the single father blame each other for their children's problems, their children escape the responsibility for their actions.

Unmotivated Children

Applications of techniques in treatment and education have become increasingly important. Tokens or poker chips have been used effectively with children from the age of 30 months to early adolescence. This "Token Economy" has been particularly popular (See "Kazdin" on pages 113-117). The reason for its popularity is that it is a powerful tool that brings forth desired behavior.

In a Token Economy, children are paid by tokens, points, or other means of specially designed symbols of merit for the completion of various academic tasks and selected social behaviors. It is important to choose an appropriate token that is difficult to be reproduced or copied by the child. The tokens can purchase a number of items including special foods, room furnishings, and clothing. Tokens or poker chips can be purchased in different sizes and colors. If you are working with more than one child in the family, a different color or size can be assigned to each child.

In order for the Token Economy to work, it must have several prerequisites. The target behaviors need to be identified, a procedure for reward must be developed, and procedures to deal with the maladaptive behavior must be in place. In some cases, there are children who appear not to care if their privileges are removed. They take a defiant stance and demonstrate no perceived response from the parents' best efforts. This type of non responsive behavior by the child results in feelings of hopelessness and misery by the parents.

Using tokens as reinforcement seems to help motivate some children who otherwise would prefer to be grounded and live without their usual privileges or pleasures. Tokens have been of tremendous usefulness in working with antisocial and delinquent youths who have committed serious offenses (See "Cohen, Filipczak, and Bis" on page 114-115). Token reinforcement can be used for youth whose behavioral patterns (such as failing grades, truancy, and running away) may lead to further decline.

Many parents who face uncaring children resort to a variety of coping responses that do not help to change the undesired behaviors. Paying children for performing specified tasks is the least recommended course of action. This is known as a one to one ratio. When children are paid directly for a prescribed behavior, such as washing cars or mowing lawns, they might take the money and run. If this happens, they remain unmotivated to discontinue undesirable behaviors or to continue desirable ones. When they are awarded with tokens, they must wait until they have earned enough tokens to receive a privilege. This could be a five-to-one or a ten-to-one ratio. There is a greater predictability for extinguishing maladaptive behavior by using token reinforcement than by paying children directly for the completion of tasks. It is very important to insure that the reward is sufficient incentive to encourage desirable behavior. Children will not be interested in working for rewards that do not appeal to them. The tasks may not be to their liking, but if they want to have specific rewards, they will have to earn them by doing the assigned duties.

"UNTREATABLES"

Unfortunately, there are those children who fall into the category of treatment resistant or "untreatables." Children of this ilk seem to lack the ability to learn from their experience and continue to repeat behaviors that get them into trouble with their parents, authority figures, peers, and law enforcement. Time and time again, these same children are sent to juvenile detention, but their uncaring behaviors that initially placed them there continue. Regardless of the consequences that they are forced to endure, they fail to learn from their mistakes and continue to repeat patterns of uncaring and unhealthy behaviors. In my clinical experience, I have found that about one of twenty children (5%) are in the category that can be labeled as "untreatables."

REVIEW OF THE TREATMENT PROCESS

The Improvement Program for Bad Children, although seemingly simple, is a process that is sometimes uncomfortable for parents. Depriving children of their privileges and pleasures might seem uncomplicated, but it can create insurmountable guilt in some parents. They are more interested in insuring their children's relief from pain and suffering than in creating discomfort for them. If children are too unhappy, parents frequently believe that they are failing as guardians. Because of that belief, they don't teach impulse control guidelines to their children.

Parent/Child Reaction

Children's initial reaction to the Improvement Program for Bad Children might be to mock the parents' attempts at correcting their behavior. They even may fool their parents by behaving properly, but this lasts for only a short time. They quickly will revert to their usual disruptive pattern of behavior.

Parents must be extremely careful at this point. In their roles as good and loving parents, they have such a desire for their children to behave well that they often will prematurely reward them for any positive sign. They also are fearful of losing their children's love if the children think that the parents are being unfair and harmful.

As stated in Chapter 3, some level of anxiety must be present if change is to occur. If a child experiences little or no discomfort, meaningful and lasting change probably will not be observed. Discomfort will occur only when the parent creates and orchestrates sufficient turmoil in their child's world. Parents must maintain strict and consistent action in the form of discipline and deprivation of privilege and pleasure, while effectively empowering the child with the power to choose. This action may precipitate a crisis, but this is the prescription for change. Remember that this is your child's crisis, not yours! It is imperative that you no longer maintain your belief that this is your problem. You can help, but this is your child's problem. This is your child's crisis.

When parents attempt to correct their children's disruptive behavior, they experience a great deal of concern for their children's well being and their genuine feelings of love. On the other hand, uncaring children are concerned only with their own happiness and comfort. As long as they are able to maintain levels of serenity without interruption, they will exhibit few problems and will make little change. It is only when expectations are presented to children that we quickly observe evidence of uncaring behaviors. You must provide children with the opportunity of behaving in a desirable manner and reaping the rewards for a "good" choice or of acting in an undesirable way and reaping those consequences. Parents must give power to their children so that they can make either choice of the following: If you choose to obey the rules, you will be allowed to have all of the pleasures and privilege that this family provides. However, if you choose not to obey the rules of this house, catastrophic consequences will follow swiftly.

Pat

Pat fits into the role of the "transformer." He basically was normal with few problems while growing up. For all intents and purposes, he was the child who was the "good boy" from the beginning. His problems did not begin until he was about twelve. At that time, he began to follow the lead of his more dominant peers. He easily was led by the stronger, more aggressive, and dominant males in his peer group. As pubescence ended and the yearnings of adolescence approached, Pat began to explore independence. Unfortunately, following the more dominant peers in his group resulted in antisocial behaviors.

During individual counseling, Pat was pleasant, agreeable, and easy to engage in conversation. Initially, he appeared interested in solving his problems, but, when he was confronted with his lack of progress, he became argumentative and abrasive. When he was asked, "What seems to be the problem?" his response was, "I have no problem. My parents do. They overreact to everything and get on my case."

Traditional psychotherapeutic techniques had little effect. Attempts to establish a working therapeutic relationship failed. Regardless of how well the relationship between Pat and me progressed, his behavior at home and school remained unchanged.

When Pat's parents began the Six Step approach, they experienced some difficulty during the first two weeks. Although they appeared motivated and enthusiastic, they reported being negligent in their efforts to comply with Step Four: Consequences. They were too quick to let Pat "off the hook" when they perceived his positive response. Obviously, Pat was able to convince his parents that he was going to do as they expected. In reality, he was forestalling his punishment.

After his parents applied Step Four in a more consistent manner, Pat reacted with anger. He attempted to ask his mother about the reasons for their reaction to his "normal" behaviors. They removed all of the items in Step Two: Privileges and Pleasures and made his penalty longer due to his continued discussion and misconduct.

After several weeks of improving and failing, they began to see a steady improvement in his overall attitude and productivity at home and at school. He quickly verbalized his unwillingness to continue to lose privileges. His parents viewed his progress as a "miracle."

Winnie

Winnie was fifteen years old and was an only child. Her occasional use of drugs and alcohol, lying, petty theft, and disobedient behavior brought her to the attention of the police, her school's counselor, her state's welfare office, and a family therapist. In spite of many conversations with the child at home and at school, she continued to evidence problems. Her parents and her school counselor were unable to gain her cooperation. Traditional individual and family psychotherapy were attempted, but failed.

From an early age, Winnie was considered to be spoiled and easily irritated. She had little interest in self-play and she was easily bored. She constantly sought her parents' attention. Attempts to redirect her actions resulted in temper tantrums. Her parents had problems in getting her to do homework. Her grades were average. At the age of eleven, her grades fluctuated between D's and F's. By the time that she was thirteen, she had lost interest in her schoolwork and was failing.

This picture is common among uncaring children. Winnie exhibited many early soft signs that her parents were untrained to observe. They were truly caring and loving parents, but they felt the usual guilt and frustration experienced by good parents. I believe that they could have been successful much earlier if they had applied the Improvement Program.

When Winnie was brought to my attention, she behaved in the same way that she had acted with her previous therapists. After trying the traditional approach without success, I suggested that the parents apply the Improvement Program for Bad Children. The target problem behaviors were:

Step One: Target Behaviors

1. drugs/alcohol
2. stealing
3. lying
4. disobedience
5. failing grades
6. temper tantrums

Step Two: Privileges and Pleasures

1. socializing with friends
2. talking on the telephone
3. watching television
4. shopping, especially for clothes

To her parents' surprise, Winnie's response was positive. During the first two weeks, her previous misbehavior ceased. I reminded them of the "honeymoon" period – the initial reaction that appears positive, but quickly is interrupted by misbehavior. After two weeks, Winnie became belligerent and defiant. They quickly reacted to her regression and imposed Step Four: Consequences. Winnie's response was to leave home. Her parents were depressed and guilt ridden. They felt that they might have been too hard on her and she might do something foolish. After much reassurance, they contacted the police and reported her as missing.

Winnie's running away from home and the subsequent parental guilt is not uncommon at this phase of intervention. The uncaring child may react to parental control by renewing and increasing her parents' feelings of guilt.

In a situation like Winnie's, parents must reinstate the original Improvement Program for Bad Children upon their children's return. If they continue to oppose their parents with dangerous behaviors, Step Four: Over Correction should be enacted. The adolescents should be told that they must perform a number of chores while they are being denied their usual privileges. Provide them with the choice to succeed or to fail. If positive results do not follow disciplinary action, the alternative is to place them in an alternative living arrangement. This could range from short term psychiatric placement to long-term residential care for behavioral disorders.

In this case, the police brought Winnie to her home. Her parents gave choices to her. She could comply with their house rules or choose to live in a state-approved residence. After having her alternatives explained, Winnie chose to comply. Although she attempted to argue and make her parents feel guilty for being so "uptight," Winnie finally settled down and did what was expected of her.

In the summary above, it is easy to see how parents can be manipulated and compelled to discontinue punitive actions. We must observe this child's running away as her reaction to her parents' mandates. She believed that, if she could confuse and obstruct her parents' actions, she could return to her previous antisocial behaviors without the fear of any consequences. Parents must be diligent and consistent in their discipline if uncaring behavior is to be treated.

Choosing A Therapist

I have alluded to the difficulty that psychotherapists have in dealing effectively with the uncaring child. Choosing an appropriate therapist is a difficult but mandatory task. The therapist must have the traditional training skills required of a child development clinician along with the added knowledge, required skills, and a genuine understanding of the "good parents" dilemma. As previously stated, the therapist too often looks for the faults of the parents and easily can miss the masked Uncaring Child Syndrome. The therapist then may turn his tactics to family therapy, which repeatedly has failed. This same pattern of failed attempts to resolve conflicts continues and results in more frustration, guilt, and suffering.

The following is a suggested list of mandatory skills needed by the psychotherapist in order to recognize, identify, and work with the uncaring child:

1. Sound knowledge of psycho social development
The therapist should be thoroughly trained in the various forces that mold human personality.

2. Experience in traditional parenting techniques
Such techniques are Parent Effectiveness Training (PET) and
Systematic Training for Effective Parenting (STEP). This
experienceis helpful in delineating the uncaring child
from the treatable child.

3. Marriage and family therapy skills
These skills are needed for the purpose of understanding
functional and dysfunctional family systems.

4. Sound knowledge of behavioral therapy techniques

5. Clear understanding of normal and abnormal child
development

6. Empathetic understanding of the family turmoil and the ability
to know the difference between "bad" parents with "bad" children
and "good" parents with "bad" children.

Those characteristics, as well as traditional knowledge and skills,
are prerequisites when choosing a psychotherapist to intervene with
your family. Obviously, because of the lack of trained therapists with
the sensitivity and understanding of the uncaring child concept, the
question arises: Where do we find such a therapist?

Through my practice in South and Central Florida, I have found a
helpful source for finding the appropriate therapist through "Toughlove",
York and York (1980). This self help program for parents who are
troubled by their children's behavior has more than 800 groups throughout the United States and Canada. The Toughlove groups with which I
am acquainted are sympathetic to parents and the problems associated
with unsuccessful therapeutic interventions, excessive financial and
emotional costs, and the tragic consequences of a fractured family.
They have had much experience with traditional psychotherapy and
have been disillusioned by the lack of positive results. Therefore, they
have developed their own referral network of agencies, therapists, at-
torneys, and treatment facilities that are especially sensitive to their
dilemmas.

Other support groups that might be considered are PET and STEP,
Gordon and Dinkmeyer (1975). I recommend these programs for help
in understanding normal and problem behavior.

Chapter 9:
Ask the Doctor

"Children today love luxury. They have bad manners, a contempt for authority, a disrespect for their elders and they like to talk instead of work. They contradict their parents, chatter before company, gobble up the best at the table, and tyrannize over their teachers."
Socrates, 500 B.C., Athens

As with any method that deals with unfamiliar territory, many questions arise from its exploration. I will attempt to answer these questions as frankly and candidly as possible. I am aware that any answer that I give about complicated issues may be incomplete and lack the full dimension that I may propose at a later date. With that in mind, I will give you the benefit of my education, experience, and research along with providing suggestions for further investigation through other sources and literature.

The following are composites of questions that have been asked by my patients throughout more than four decades of my therapy sessions.

1. What causes the Uncaring Child Syndrome?

I believe that the Uncaring Child Syndrome is constitutional. In other words, it involves inherited elements that are transmitted to the child. I believe that these kids have a predisposition to certain behaviors and personality traits.

Some evidence suggests the XYY syndrome (a genetic disorder in which individuals possess an extra male chromosome) produces a genetic predisposition for crime. These individuals may not commit violent crimes, but they do tend to commit minor offenses.

When there are several children in the family and only one turns out "bad," how do we explain the remaining members' positive outcomes? In spite of the parents' repeated attempts to solve these conflicts, the uncaring child remains unchanged. The explanation cannot be dismissed as the result of the child's position as the youngest, middle, or oldest sibling in the family. Neither can we continue to blame the parents, especially when there is evidence that they are blameless. This is not to say that no evidence suggests that certain parents cause messed-up kids. I have seen many kids who have come from abusive parents. The results of bad parenting are well documented. This is not the case with "good parents" rearing unresponsive, uncaring children. It is time that we look more closely at these children and shift the responsibility to them when appropriate.

2. What are the earliest signs of the Uncaring Child Syndrome?

Early warning signs are offered in Chapter Four as soft signs. The earliest signs can be seen about the age of two. The complaints heard most often are: "He doesn't listen to me." "She rarely finishes what she begins. " "Noises or people easily distract him." "She has difficulty in keeping her mind on what she is doing." "He is impulsive." "I can't turn my back on her." "He has no patience." "She fidgets." "He can't play alone." "She's hyper, gets upset, and displays her temper if things don't go her way." "He's disobedient." "She has little or no regard for the rights of others." "He's oppositional, easily upset, accident-prone, demanding, manipulative, and defiant." "She has sudden mood swings, expects others to indulge her, takes unnecessary risks, blames others, denies wrongdoing, and seeks the forbidden." "He has the knack for forgetfulness." "She holds contempt for advice."

It continues to amaze me that a child so young has the ingredients of so many characteristics of an older child. Because of this understanding of the importance of early developmental signs, I advise parents to look at these soft signs as red flags that alert us to potential problems. If we can be alerted early enough, we may correct certain undesirable behavior before it becomes more severe or irreversible.

3. Are their any soft signs for the infant or toddler?

In some of the children's actions, we may see soft signs at an earlier age, but it is not until about the age of two that we begin to see a more consistent pattern. Prior to that age, their behavior is at the exploratory level. Trying to identify soft signs before that age would be confusing and probably misleading.

4. I am the mother of a six year old boy. He has had behavioral problems since he was two. My pediatrician told me, "He will grow out of it." What do you think?

Ever since I can remember, pediatricians, professional counselors, and other advice giving professionals have been saying to parents, "They will grow out of it," for a variety of complaints about behavior. I believe that we should look at any behavior that concerns us if it persists for more than two weeks. I do not believe that problem behavior merely disappears by children growing out of it. My experience has been to the contrary. Behaviors that persist for more than two weeks in spite of attempts to change them often develop into more serious behaviors. For example, a child who lies now about doing homework might lie later about his whereabouts, drinking, or stealing.

5. Do you find any specific medical problems with uncaring children?

I rarely have associated any medical problems with uncaring children. These children seem to be in the same physical health, both medically and neurologically, as most "normal" children.

6. Do children who are labeled with Attention Deficit Hyperactivity Disorder also possess characteristics of UCS?

I do find that many children with the label of ADHD have similarities to uncaring children in their early behavior. They may exhibit inattention, restless movement, distractibility, poor concentration, hyperactivity, and impulsivity. However, their capacity to feel subjective anxiety separates them from the uncaring child. Therefore, I do not see a relationship between those children who have ADHD and those who have UCS merely because they have characteristics of both.

To illustrate this point further, let us look at the following portrait. Billy is an eight year old who has problems finishing the things that he starts. He has trouble listening, concentrating, playing by himself, and organizing his schoolwork. He is hyperactive and he is beginning to lie about doing his homework.

When Billy's school counselor suggested that he might have ADHD, a specialized program at school was initiated. As the problems associated with ADHD were being addressed at home and at school, his lying behavior stopped. Billy's parents remarked that they always believed that he felt guilt and remorse for his lying.

The above picture always is different when dealing with the uncaring child. If Billy were an uncaring child, we would see a host of other misbehaviors associated with the syndrome, such as blaming others, defiance, selfishness, lack of learning from experience, lack of guilt or remorse, and unresponsiveness to parents. His response would be negative to almost every attempt to correct his behavior.

7. What will the children become when they are adults?

When an uncaring child begins to pursue antisocial behavior, it is remarkable how rarely they will change course. The uncaring child who has grown into an adult is poorly equipped to deal with the responsibilities of a male/female relationship and even less able to rear children. They are unable to be intimate in relationships although they may give the appearance of intimacy to their observers. Much like the person with Borderline Personality Disorder (See "American Psychiatric Association" on pages 83-85.), they may be impulsive or unpredictable, unstable and intense in their interpersonal relationships, or demonstrate intense anger or lack of control. They could be emotionally unstable with shifts in mood. They may have bouts of suicidal or homicidal ideas or gestures. Just as they are unable to adopt healthy standards, goals, values, or ideals, they are almost impotent in developing empathy, genuineness, warmth, or respect in intimate relationships.

Some of these individuals actually will appear to be making improvements in their lives by adopting newly formed roles. These new roles may come in several forms, such as religious conversion or job status, but the individuals will maintain their uncaring behaviors.

8. I am the parent of a fifteen year old girl. She refuses to listen to me. She's failing all of her subjects at school. She's disrespect-

ful. I believe that she is using drugs. I have tried cutting off all of her privileges, but she sneaks out of the house late at night. I have received calls from the school about her lack of attendance. We tried counseling, but that was a joke. Nothing that we have tried has worked. What can I do?

The first thing that you have to ask yourself is, "How far am I willing to go?" Although it is impossible for me to know clearly if she is an uncaring child, the treatment suggested is much the same as it would be for any child with extreme behavior. Would you be willing to put your child in a residential facility for an undetermined length of time? If you use this step merely as a threat and have no intention of proceeding, your child quickly sees it as an invitation to further her antisocial behavior.

Let us suppose that you have followed the treatment program as outlined in Chapter 8. If your child's misbehavior continues, I recommend placement in a residential facility, not only to control her misbehavior, but also to prevent any harm from coming to her or others. You calmly could tell your child that you are in the process of locating a residential placement for her. However, when you make that statement, you must proceed if she calls your bluff. If she is willing to work on changing the misbehaviors (as outlined in Chapter 8), then residential placement can be avoided.

9. How can I get my children to understand that they are responsible for their own behavior?

It is essential for you to make it perfectly clear that it is your children's choice either to continue their misbehaviors or to terminate them. Also, they must know that it is their choice whether they gain or lose privileges. You are providing them with empowerment to succeed or to fail. This takes away the perception that the children's poor behaviors are the parents' fault. Remember that it is the children's discomfort that eventually will make them desire to change. Parents must initiate/produce controlled discomfort in their children because they do not feel any form of anxiety beyond the moment. Always place the responsibility of their behaviors on the children themselves.

10. How do you deal with a child who does not care if you take her privileges away or seems to lack any concern about being grounded or receiving any other restrictions?

Periodically, I see a child who challenges the family or appears ambivalent. A battle of nerves is fought by the child's passive/aggressive nature.

In this battle, the child accepts her parents' response to her behavior. Instead of making any attempt to regain her privileges, she concedes to the punishment. The child's passive response leads to utter frustration by her parents. They feel hopeless and angered by the child's passive restraint and lack of concern.

After you strip the child of all of her privileges and she appears to have accepted total grounding, make a list of household chores for her to complete. The completion of each chore would grant homebound privileges only. She is not to have any out of home privileges until all of the chores have been completed. In this way, you will be attempting to regain her cooperation by meaningful activity. The Token Economy referenced in Chapter 8: Unmotivated Children is a highly recommended technique for these children.

11. I have a twenty-year-old son who has had a behavior problem most of his life. He always has been unreliable and untruthful. He is an alcoholic who has been sober for two weeks. Between therapists and rehabilitation programs, I have spent a fortune for his recovery. The longest time that he has been sober is three months. He says that he is working and needs a car and insurance so that he can maintain his job. I always have helped him in the past, but have felt manipulated. I am afraid not to help him now. What should I do?

This appears to be a case of co-dependency. Your continued efforts to help your son is a rescue mission. The responsibility of sobriety is his, not yours. You first must make known your limits and expectations if you are going to assist him. He regularly must attend an Alcoholics Anonymous (AA) program. If necessary, he should be in an alcohol rehabilitation program. He then must maintain sobriety for six months before you consider assisting him.

It is essential that you discontinue further financial support without his sobriety and participation in AA for a period of six months. This places the full responsibility of his recovery on him, not you. The only measure of his recovery is what he does, not what he says. When he has fulfilled your expectations, you may consider trusting his word, at least for this particular episode. After the six-month period of his consistent participation in his recovery, you then can assist him with progressive and measured support. However, be careful that you do not sabotage his progress by another emotional and financial rescue. Go slow and easy with your support. Remember that you have been the "sucker" before and it is easy to rekindle the past co dependent behavior.

Discontinue feeding the fire of abnormal behavior and feed only the momentum of success. Your attempts to rescue and provide for your child will allow him to continue feeding off of you without giving back. Parasitic actions are common not only by the addictive personality, but also by the uncaring child.

12. What do "bad" parents do that is wrong?

Most psychotherapists consider "bad" parents as those who cause problems in their children through their own inadequacies or harmful behavior. They may be rejecting, abusive, deviant, or traumatizing. This does not mean that these parents are unable to change their bad behavior. With the help of family therapy and the proper motivation, the outcome may be positive.

13. If I discipline my daughter too much, I am afraid that she will run away, use drugs, or take up with sleazy characters.

First of all, we must evaluate the toll that misbehavior takes. It disturbs the lives of those who are involved with the uncaring child. If this behavior goes unchecked, the results can be devastating. In spite of your fears of losing your child "to the street," you must take charge while attempting to redirect her misguided and destructive energy. If the child chooses to live on the street, we must choose options to meet the crisis. These options may include the police or the department of children and youth protective services. You must not become intimidated by your child's threat of fleeing. You must take a stand and, considering the circumstances, know that you are doing the best that you can.

14. My teenage son punches and kicks holes in the wall when he gets mad. He is verbally abusive, makes threats to leave home, and blames us for his unhappiness. What do you suggest that we do?

The first thing I would recommend is to contact a family therapist who has a clear understanding of behavioral therapy and family system skills. The therapist could determine the presence of an emotional illness or the formation of symptoms that may account for his behavior. If this intervention fails to uncover, mediate, and resolve his behavior, I would then review and implement the Improvement Program for Bad Children as outlined in Chapter 8. If he is not evidencing any symptoms of depression, the Six Step approach may be extremely useful in extinguishing his maladaptive behavior.

15. My sixteen-year-old daughter has threatened to kill herself on two occasions, but she has never attempted to do it. Should I take her threat of suicide seriously?

Yes! Absolutely! Many suicidal individuals will feel suicidal for only a brief period. When these individuals contemplate killing themselves, they are feeling worse than they ever have before and they want to stop that horrible pain at any cost. It is essential that you take a suicide threat seriously. Your daughter's verbal warning indicates a serious threat and should not be taken casually. If it is determined that her threats are bogus, hospitalization should be considered as an appropriate response. It is equally important to have your daughter understand that her threat of suicide will always be taken seriously and, therefore, her threats may result in the loss of her freedoms when she is committed to the crisis unit of a psychiatric inpatient hospital. By making her understand that you are serious, you will be taking away the possibility of her using her threat as a manipulative weapon.

16. My boy is four years old. Is he too young for me to begin working on his temper outbursts?

Definitely not. I believe that you can work on changing misbehavior as soon as children are able to understand what you are saying. When a child begins to explore areas of the house that might be dangerous, it is important to let them know which boundaries are safe and which are dangerous. If you stop children from putting their hands on a hot stove, you are teaching the same principal to them. You should be teaching ideals, standards, and goals to your children during their entire early development. Even temper tantrums are socially unacceptable because they infringe on the rights of others. Therefore, immediately begin working to change his behavior.

17. My husband and I are the parents of three children. The middle child is making us crazy by refusing to do chores, leaving his room in a mess, lying, and constantly having problems at school. He seems unconcerned with our feelings and I am convinced that he takes no responsibility for any of his actions. My other two children are fine and cause few problems. My concern is that I am spending most of my time with the middle child and feel that I am neglecting the others. Also, I don't know if I am doing more harm than good. My husband and I are either spending many hours talking to him or grounding him. We are feeling guilt, frustration, and anger. We no longer know what is the right thing to do. Please help!

I advise you to find a family therapist who is skilled in behavioral therapy and family systems skills. Family issues that may be creating the problem need to be explored and resolved. It is important for the rest of the family to have a realistic view of what your child's behavior is doing to each person individually and to the family as a whole. Allow him and the rest of the family to take responsibility for their choices. Make the consequences of their choices clear. As parents of a misbehaving and possibly uncaring child, you must deal with him in a relaxed and guiltless manner. His defiant, selfish, and indifferent attitude makes him almost impossible to reach. Guilt, therefore, is a waste of time and energy. Stop talking about gaining his cooperation. Stop talking about attempting to make him feel guilt or remorse for his actions. This is the time to act, not to talk. Allow him to experience the consequences of his choices regardless of how long it takes. If he chooses to disregard your expectations, act on the consequences as discussed in Chapter 8.

18. I'm the mother of a thirteen year old girl who has been a behavioral problem since my remarriage two years ago. My husband insists that she is spoiled and that I am inconsistent in my parenting. He is always on her case for chores, homework, and minor misbehaviors. I'm worried that my marriage may break up if this continues. What should I do?

This appears to be a common problem with remarriage. Since the 1980's, the divorce rate has spiraled upwards. Previously, parents were told to, "Act as one voice. Come to a mutual agreement about discipline for the child. Do not allow the child to get between you and your spouse."

Although this is good advice for biological parents, it usually is not applicable for those who have remarried. Because of the disruption to the family's stability and established roles, the new spouse must be aware of the previous roles of the family members and must resist changing that structure.

Remember that this family existed prior to the new member's arrival. The new member must not overshadow the biological parent when it comes to raising children. The only time that I advise new members of remarried families to intervene is when the behavior of the children interferes directly with their lives or personal space. For example, if a child uses his stepfather's tools without permission, the stepfather has the right to discuss this with the child. However, both parents should discuss any disciplinary actions. The biological parent should be the only one who deals with the discipline. Children may resent a new member's dominant role, which may make them feel displaced.

19. I have gotten calls from the school about my twelve year old son's terrible behavior. They say that he is disrupting the class by his interruptions, noises, and general clowning. He has difficulty in finishing his work and might fail most of his subjects. He is not a big problem at home, but he does tease his seven year old sister too much. What help can you offer?

To understand the roots of this problem, several issues need to be considered. We first must determine the possibility of a learning disorder and/or attention deficit with or without a hyperactivity condition. This usually can be accomplished by psychological testing at school. Children may cover up their weaknesses by misbehaving. Then, I would handle the teasing behavior by using the Improvement Program for Bad Children as outlined in Chapter 8. The following summary may be helpful:

Step One: Target Behavior
Teasing his sister

Step Two: Privileges and Pleasures
List his privileges and pleasurable activities

Step Three: Warning
Inform child of consequence if behavior persists

Step Four: Consequence
Removal of three favorite privileges from Step Two

Step Five: Over Correction
Additional chores while being grounded if the behavior does not improve

Step Six: Reward
Reward for not teasing. Saying "thank you" or simply expressing your appreciation is sufficient. Do not "over-reward."

20. My sixteen year old son admits that he smokes marijuana. He says that this drug is safe and will do no harm. He is managing to do average schoolwork and is not creating any serious problems at home. I'm still concerned about him and fear the worst. If I try to ground him or punish him, I'm afraid that he will leave home and live on the street.

There are several problems associated with your son's behavior. First: Marijuana is illegal. He is breaking the law by smoking the drug. Second: There is a downside after any amount of use. It includes decreased eye/hand coordination, which makes driving and operating other mechanical devices unsafe. There is evidence that the use of marijuana can cause problems to respiratory, endocrine, and immune systems. There is a greater risk of cancer due to marijuana than to cigarettes. Additionally, in spite of ill-informed claims to the contrary, marijuana is addictive.

If you need further indication that marijuana is injurious to our youth, be reminded that its use may decrease motivation. It also lessens interest in educational and career pursuits that we as parents expect and demand from our offspring.

In addition, your son is not living up to the expectations of the family. As the parent, you have the right to set rules, regulations, standards, goals, and principals for the child. You do not have to accept his edicts that replace common sense, morality, and good judgment. I advise you to make a serious issue of his smoking marijuana in the attempt to extinguish this illegal behavior. Approach the issue in the same way that you would approach any serious misbehavior.

You may need to look into a drug rehabilitation program in order to break the bond of the addictive elements of his drug use. If he remains resistive to treatment, consider the possibility of treatment through involuntary commitment procedures or your state's department of children and youth services.

21. Does psychiatric treatment help the child?

Psychotherapy and psychotropic medications have not made an impact in treating uncaring children primarily because they do not have the ability to learn from past experiences and also because some counselors are not adequately trained nor skilled in working with these special individuals. These children repeat unhealthy behavior regardless of the consequences. They continuously blame others for their misfortune. They are unreliable, untruthful, and insincere. Although they may give the appearance of responding positively to therapy, their past unhealthy patterns can reappear.

In working with the uncaring child, I find it more useful to work with the parents rather than with the child, unless the child truly is willing to work on relevant issues. When I am able to readjust and realign parental thinking and behavior, therapy becomes more useful for the child. When the child begins to experience discomfort because of the parents' intrusion in his life, he or she may be more agreeable to working with a therapist.

22. Do uncaring children come from specific socioeconomic levels?

No. These kids come from every socioeconomic and environmental background. Children who evidence uncaring behaviors may come from any family, rich or poor.

23. Does genetic or inherited predisposition have any bearing on uncaring children?

It is my belief that genetic and inherited predispositions have a great deal to do with their uncaring behaviors. Many children behave in ways that are unexplainable to parents. For example, Joey pulls the wings off of butterflies. When he is questioned or reprimanded by his parents, he simply reacts without shame, guilt, or remorse. His responses lack the genuine feelings that would be expected from a feeling, sensitive, and caring human being. In contrast, Joey's behavior is confusing and perplexing for his parents who have evidenced love and affection for their children.

To fully understand Joey's behavior, we may need to examine the backgrounds of members of Joey's nuclear and extended family to determine the roots of this maladaptive psychopathological behavior. There may be some distant relative who has had a causative relationship or inherited (genetic) predisposition to explain Joey's behavior.

24. Do uncaring children come primarily from alcoholic families and do they have a greater tendency of becoming alcoholics?

I have not seen any evidence that alcoholic families are a primary source of uncaring children. Moreover, I have not observed that this group turns to alcohol any more or any less than "normal" children do. Throughout my clinical experience, I have not seen any direct relationship between alcoholism and the uncaring child.

25. Why is it so difficult for these children to stop their behavior?

Not only do these kids have difficulty in learning from past experiences, they also appear to be addicted to their behaviors. They display many of the compulsive behaviors of the alcoholic, drug addict, sex offender, and compulsive overeater. They cannot stop. They appear to be consumed by an inner force that cannot be penetrated by the outside world. This driving and unyielding energy seems to have a will of its own. Psychologically, uncaring children are addicts. Their addictions are to their misbehaviors. Their misbehaviors are like the alcoholics' liquor. When confronted by their constant bad actions, they promise that they will never repeat such behaviors, but they invariably do.

26. Do I need to see a therapist for my child's problem behavior or can I do this on my own?

I recommend that you first attempt to change your child's misbehavior by learning basic childrearing techniques. They can be learned from many self help books about parenting. (See my references at the end of this book.) Also, a parent-training group in your school, church, or community might be helpful.

I also recommend that you engage a child and family therapist if the target behavior continues and causes problems to increase within the family. A child/family therapist or psychiatrist must be contacted if your child shows evidence of depression, suicidal thoughts or gestures, or any other signs that need to be evaluated. The family therapist should evaluate other motivational factors that may be causing your child to act in an irrational manner. In any case, it is important to know the entire story of what may be taking place in your child's life that causes disturbing or disruptive behavior.

27. I have a twenty two year-old daughter living at home. After she finished high school, she worked at a few jobs for brief periods of time. She was always a lazy and poorly motivated student. Although she is not working now, she says that she is looking for work. I am reluctant to give money to her, but she needs gas to look for work. My husband yells at me for giving the money and she is the source of many of our arguments. I always seem to be between my husband and my daughter. I think I'm doing the right thing, but I'm not sure.

This appears to be an issue of poorly defined family roles and expectations. Your daughter expects and is provided with essential money, food, and lodging. Her lack of ambition and motivation has been obvious for a long time, so this has become her expected behavioral pattern. As her maladaptive behavior persists, you and your husband remain in conflict.

I suggest that you and your husband clarify your own expectations of your daughter's role in the family. Is it okay for her to live with you without appropriate expectations? Is it acceptable for her not to have a job or career? Consider requiring her to make choices. You could say, "In exchange for gas money, we expect you to contribute to the household by doing household duties." When she is unemployed, you can assign major household responsibilities. However, when she is employed, you should require that she makes financial contributions to the family.

This plan decreases the possibility of her skirting her responsibility to the family and makes her role much clearer. The conflict between you and your husband also should decrease.

28. My son just turned 28. Since he was 19, he has been in and out of prison for possession of drugs, grand theft auto, and burglary. He has been in conflict with society since he was eight. Whenever he gets into trouble, he is always drunk. Throughout the years, my

entire family has been bailing him out of one jam or another. Nothing seems to help. He is ripping us apart. What do you advise?

Your child appears to have turned his early misbehaviors into adult antisocial criminal behaviors. Children of this type ignore any consequences of their misconducts. Even when an extreme form of consequence results (such as prison), these children continue with their destructive behaviors and seemingly are void of good judgment and remorse.

I believe in the concept of "letting go." This is a state of mind in which you are no longer involved emotionally with the individual who continues to resist and refuses to adjust to normal social standards. This will be achieved when you are able to say to your son, "I will no longer support you in any way whatsoever, financially or emotionally, until you gain meaningful employment and stay out of trouble for a period of six months. At that time, I will reevaluate your progress and my relationship with you."

Of course, this stance is difficult for any parent. The very thought of disconnecting from a loved one is frightful. "No matter what, a mother is there for her child" is the motto of mothers throughout this country. Fear of "abandoning" their offspring makes mothers resist the thought of letting go.

However, if you look at the process of letting go more clearly, you will understand that you are not abandoning your child. You will "be there" for him when he makes the decision to "be there" for himself. When he chooses behavior that is healthy and discontinues his unloving and destructive conduct, you then can choose to be there for him. In this way, both of you have choices to make. This time, however, you are clear and have a specific time frame for evaluating his progress and making future plans.

I feel that it is important to discuss another process that is totally undesirable and possibly destructive for parents to perform. This is the process of "cutting off." Unlike the process of "letting go," when you have given certain choices for your child to consider before having the opportunity of regaining your support, "cutting off" is when you no longer provide any choice for your child to return. It is the final decree to your child when you say, "You are no longer welcome in our home – no matter what." Some families have said to their children, "You are dead and no longer exist in our minds." In my opinion, the process of cutting off leaves the family damaged. The act of cutting off is replete with hate and revenge. There can be little justification for this action and it may result in irreversible harm.

29. I am a widowed mother of a 36 year-old divorced son. He uses all kinds of drugs and associates with undesirable individuals. His behavior began when he was in high school. He is constantly calling me or coming over to my house to ask for money. I always attempt to persuade him to seek professional help. His usual reply is, "I don't need any. I'll be all right. Don't worry about me." He is currently working as a cook, but he rarely holds a job for more than six months. I know he uses the money I give him for drugs, but I feel so guilty when I don't give it to him. Nothing I do seems to work. Is there some advice you can give me to assist my son?

This is certainly a sad and devastating situation, but it is not uncommon. You appear to fit the profile of a co-dependent. Your continued financial support is your contribution to his psychopathological personality disturbance. Although giving him money eases your guilt to some degree, it provides a "source of food" for his unending addictive hunger.

My first advice is to locate an anonymous alcoholics and/or narcotics support group for the families of addicts, such as AL-Anon or Nar-Anon. They will aid and support you in your effort to discourage your son's denial system. At the very least, they will offer assistance in stopping your behavior that helps you to sustain your son's use of drugs.

My second advice is for you to understand that, when you begin to improve your behavior, your son's behavior may worsen. He may become agitated or depressed. Your usual guilt reaction might be to give in to him as you have in the past. With your support group, you will have knowledgeable people at your side to assist in your progress.

30. I have a son who throws temper tantrums and won't settle down while in restaurants or shopping malls? What should I do?

On many occasions in restaurants, I have seen parents disciplining their child for fooling around, shouting, throwing food, or having a temper outburst. Frustrated and angry because of their child's lack of a positive response, parents sometimes resort to yelling, threatening, or striking their child. Faced with the glares of other patrons and upset by their helplessness and inability to cope with their child, the parents either become impotent in dealing with the situation or resort to inappropriate and sometimes destructive behavior. Sometimes, parents simply do not know alternate methods of managing difficult behavior.

When talking, reasoning, and traditional child raising techniques fail to produce the desired behavior, I suggest measures that are designed to stop the child's misbehavior immediately.

You can eliminate the behavior through use of the "Restroom Intervention." If you are in a restaurant and your simple requests fail to stop your child's disruptive behavior, quickly remove him from the table or wherever his misbehavior is taking place. Usher him to the nearest restroom and discuss his misconduct. In a calm and firm manner, reassure him of your love and respect for him, but let him know that any further incident will result in removal from wherever the problem is taking place. If he persists in misconduct when you return, take him home for further disciplinary action. This action should be in accordance with the Improvement Program for Bad Children in Chapter 8.

I have received a lot of positive feedback from parents who have used Restroom Intervention. I believe that the results are due to the unusual environment in which the confrontation takes place. The compulsive action is interrupted, which leaves the youngster unsettled and more receptive to your request. The child is very much aware of his new surroundings and feels intimidated by the comings and goings of the individuals in the restroom.

Another technique that works well with this situation is what I call "Precipitating a Crisis." This technique involves a designated family member or friend who is part of the strategy and is prepared to intervene if your child has a tantrum. Then create a situation that usually sets in motion the ingredients for a full-blown temper outburst. When the outburst occurs, warn the child (Step 3) that you will remove him from the activity. If the warning fails to gain your child's compliance, take the child to the home of the designated person. After enjoying the rest of the afternoon with your family, take all of them with you when you pick up your son. Let your uncaring child see your family's smiling faces showing that the pleasurable event that took place in spite of his absence. This technique allows the child to understand that you mean business and can be relied upon to act on your demands. The child will learn that, unless he complies with reasonable family demands and rules, he quickly will lose the pleasures and privileges that are granted to other family members.

Conclusion

On the surface, your uncaring child seems simply to lack discipline. The misbehavior of most "normal" children generally diminishes when parents learn about common behavioral problems and apply the effective techniques. To the contrary, the uncaring child's misbehavior usually continues. Parents then experience an abundance of unhealthy feelings that leave them impotent in resolving the parent/child conflict.

To understand uncaring children, you first must be clear about the difference between good and bad parents and between good and bad children. This concept is crucial in working with uncaring children. The parents' act of "rescuing" their children is ineffective behavior and is commonly attempted by "good" parents who are trying to help their children. However, "bad" parents commonly cause bad behavior in most of their sons and daughters.

With a comprehensive understanding of the Uncaring Child Syndrome and enhanced resources, parents will be better prepared to take charge and finally see positive behavioral changes in their children.

All of us who influence young people must continue to work with expectations of positive growth, regardless of the children's diagnoses. In spite of their difficult nature, individuals with the Uncaring Child Syndrome usually have a chance for improvement. Like antisocial adults, these children may mellow and their uncaring behavior might subside as they grow older. Some of these children have been known to improve as a result of sheer parental tenacity.

Mothers, fathers, and guardians, do not give up on your uncaring child. As good parents, you must remain in charge, implement a successful behavioral program, and provide consistent guidance to healthy choices. Most importantly, always remember that the responsibilities and outcomes of those choices belong solely to your child – not to you!

REFERENCES*
and
RECOMMENDED READING

* American Psychiatric Association. (1994). *Diagnostic and statistical manual of mental disorders.* (4th ed.) Washington, DC: American Psychiatric Association.

Ardrey, R. (1962) African Genesis; A Personal Investigation into the Animal Origins and Nature of Man. New York: Atheneum.

Bennett, W.J. (1986). What Works: *Schools without drugs.* U.S. Department of Education.

Bernstein, S. (2000). *10 Days to a Less Defiant Child.* New York, New York: Marlowe & Company.

Bugliosi, V. (1974). *Helter Skelter.* New York: Norton.

* Chapman, A.H. (1976). *Harry Stack Sullivan: His Life and His Work.* New York: G.P. Putnam's Sons. Page 114.

Chapman, A.H. (1976). *Textbook of Clinical Psychiatry.* (2nd ed.). Philadelphia/Toronto: J.B. Lippincott Co.

Cleckley, H. (1976). *The Mask of Sanity.* St. Louis: C.V. Mosby Co.

* Cohen, H.L., Filipezak, J.A., & Bis, J.S. (1968) In Kazdin, A.E. (1997). *The Token Economy.* New York: Plenum Press. Page 114.

* Dinkmeyer, D. (1976). *Systematic Training for Effective Parenting.* Minnesota: American Guidance Service.

Fossey, D. (1979). "Development of the Mountain Gorilla" in D.A. Hamburg & E.R. McCown (Eds.), *The Great Apes.* Menlo Park, CA: Benjamin/Cummings.

Franks, C. F. and Wilson, G. T. (1974). *Annual Review of Behavior Therapy Theory & Practice.* New York: Brunner/Mazel.

Freud, S. (1923). *The Ego and the Id.* London: Hogarth Press.

Ginott, H.G. (1965). *Between Parent & Child.* New York: Avon Books.

Goodall, J. (1986). *The Chimpanzees of Gombe: patterns of behavior.* Cambridge, Mass and London, England: The Belknap Press of Harvard University Press.

* Gordon, T. (1975). *P.E.T.* New York: New American Library.

Green, R.W. (2001). *The Explosive Child.* New York, New York: Harper Collins.

Harlow, H.F. (1958). *The nature of love.* American Psychologist. 13.

Harrell, T.H.; Honaker, L.M. and Gibson, K.D. (1984). *Child & Adolescent Diagnostic Screening Inventory.* Indialantic, FL: Psychologistics, Inc.

Jersild, A.T. (1963). *The Psychology of Adolescence.* New York/London: MacMillan Co.

* Kazdin, A.E. (1977). *The Token Economy.* New York: Plenum Press.

* Kinkead, E. (1959). (1st ed. reprinted 1981). *In Every War But One.* Westport, Connecticut: Greenwood Press.

Kleindienst, L. (1994, January 1). "New year brings new laws." The Orlando Sentinel. Pages A1 and A14.

Klineman, G.; Butler, S. and Conn, D. (1980). *The Cult That Dies: Tragedy of Jim Jones and the Peoples Temple.* New York: Putnam.

Lindholm, C. (2000). Culture and Identity: The History, Theory, and Practice of Psychological Anthropology, New York: McGraw-Hill.

* Meltz, B. (1994, March 25). "Children must come first, book tells policymakers." *The Miami Herald.* Pages 1F and 2F.

Maslow, A.H. (1936). "A theory of sexual behavior in infra human primates." *Journal of Genet Psychology.* Volume 48.

Maslow, A.H. (1960). "Some parallels between sexual and dominance behavior of infra human primates and the fantasies of patients in psychotherapy." *Journal of Nervous and Mental Disease.* Vol. 131.

* Perls, F.; Hefferline, R.R. and Goodman, P. (1951). *Gestalt Therapy.* New York: Julian Press.

Raine, A. (1993). *The Psychopathology of Crime: Criminal behavior as a clinical disorder.* New York: Academic Press, a division of Harcourt Brace.

* Reid, W.H. (1978). *The Psychopath.* New York

Rogers, C.R. (1951). *Client Centered Therapy.* Boston: Houghton Mifflin.

Samenow, S.E. (1984). *Inside The Criminal Mind*. New York: The New York Times Book Co., Times Books.

Savitz, L.D. and Johnston, N. (1978). *Crime in Society*. New York: Wiley & Sons.

* Schjelderup-Ebbe, T. (1922). *Beitrage zur sozialpsycholo gie des haushuhns*. Z Psychol. Vol. 88. Pages 225 and 252.

Skinner, B.F. (1953). *Science and Human Behavior*. New York: MacMillan.

Spitz, R. (1965). *The First Year of Life*. New York: International Universities Press.

* Staats, A.W. and Staats, C.K. (1963). *Complex Human Behavior*. New York: Reinehart & Winston.

Sullivan, H.S. (1954). *The Psychiatric Interview*. New York: W.W. Norton & Company.

Talmadge, D. and Theler, J. (2004). *The Ephraim's Child: Characteristics, Capabiities, and Challenges of Children Who Are Intensely More*. Springville, Utah: Horizon Publishers.

Turecki, S. (1985, 1989, 2000). *The Difficult Child.* New York: Bantam Books.

Weisberg, L.W. and Greenberg R. (1991). *When Acting Out Isn't Acting.* New York: Bantam Books.

* Wolpe, J.L. (1969). *The Practice of Behavior Therapy.* New York: Pergamon Press.

* York, P. and York, D. (1980). *Toughlove.* Sellersville, PA: Community Service Foundation.

About the Author

Dr. Hoffman has a full-time private practice in Ormond Beach, Florida, where he is a licensed marriage and family therapist and a mental health counselor.

Dr. Hoffman began his work at the Devereux Foundation in 1963 and specialized as a music therapist for children. In 1969, he completed a one-year clinical internship at the Menninger Memorial Hospital in Kansas. That experience led to his first book, Hear the Music! A New Approach to Mental Health. His work in the field of organic brain damage led to The Hoffman Organicity Test.

A results-oriented and powerful presenter, Dr. Hoffman leads informative "how-to" workshops that provide effective and measurable techniques to improve and to enhance the forensic skills of mental health professionals.

He is a past clinical member of the American Association for Marriage & Family Therapy and is certified by the National Board for Clinical Counselors. He is the clinical director of the Counseling & Psychotherapy Center in Ormond Beach and the president of the National Board of Forensic Evaluators.

Beginning in 1976 during his work at the Hazleton/Nanticoke MH/MR Center in Pennsylvania, Dr. Hoffman assisted in development, training, and child custody evaluations between the mental health center and the Luzerne/Wyoming County Circuit Court. He is an expert witness in the fields of forensic mental health evaluations, child custody disputes, and competency assessments throughout the United States.

AUTHORS NOTE

Advice to parents: *"At age thirteen, seal the teenager in a barrel and leave a hole at the top for air and for the sending of food through a straw. Then, at age sixteen, Plug up the hole! -Mark Twain-*

In all my years as a child development specialist I observed that for certain groups of children, those designated as suffering from attention deficit disorder (ADD), Autism, and other non-specific childhood disorders, the availability of special resources required for the accomplishment of this goal is extremely limited.

Not since the 60's has there been a comprehensive assessment, diagnostic and treatment approach that encompassed the utilization of a highly specialized team of mental health professionals dedicated to the overall continuity care of the child. The current trend in the United States, when it comes to treating very difficult children, is to view them as "treatment resistive" and treated by counselors with limited or no specialized child development training, education or experience. Therefore, when all is said and done, the parents remain frustrated, guilt ridden, and without any meaningful direction to turn. Because of inadequate, substandard assessment and treatment, the parents are also left with feelings of hopelessness, helplessness and haplessness.

The Hoffman Institute, (HI) located in Daytona Beach, Florida, was developed to serve families by providing specialized assessments and treatment plans for parents of difficult children. This is accomplished through a professional team approach used to assess and diagnose attention deficit hyperactivity disorders, autism, disruptive behaviors, oppositional defiant disorders, and various other problematic child behavioral issues.

The HI clinicians specialize in the assessment, diagnoses and treatment of childhood disorders. Parents come to HI with the assurance that they will be provided the highest quality of professional care by a team approach. Each clinical team member is highly educated, trained and experienced in the assessment, diagnoses and treatment of childhood disorders. The family will be evaluated with the emphasis on "how to" implement meaningful strategies and methods of effective parenting, not merely "why" the child is behaving as they do, or "what" caused the problem. Although it is important to know why the child acts as they do, and what caused them to do so, it is paramount to offer parents specific steps and a plan when they are home with their child, and what to do when they are at school. Also included in this form of intervention would be special consultation with schools and teachers by knowledgeable physicians, social workers, psychologists, education specialists, language specialists, behavior-shaping technologists, and others.

It is with this dedicated effort, by a team of highly trained professionals, HI has undertaken an authentic and comprehensive approach to the total mental health care of the child.

For single copies or bulk purchases of
This and other books by
Norman E. Hoffman, Ph.D.

Send your payment to:
VG PRESS
595 W. Granada Blvd., Suite H
Ormond Beach, Florida 32174

or call:
(1-386-677-3995)

or order online:
http://www.nbfe.net/books.htm

One book: $19.95
plus postage and handling: 3.95
The total is: $23.90

If you are ordering by mail within the United States,
Please add $21.20 for each additional book ordered
At the same time. (This price already includes $1.25
for postage and handling.) For the mailing costs for
non-USA deliveries, please send an email that includes
the name of your country to drnorm@nbfe.net.

Please allow two to four weeks for delivery within the
United States. Please email to learn if the price or postage
has changed.